CHECK
YOUR TAX
THE
COMPLETE GUIDE
2011–2012

CHECK YOUR TAX

THE
COMPLETE GUIDE
2011–2012

by

GRAHAM M KITCHEN, FCA

foulsham
LONDON • NEW YORK • TORONTO • SYDNEY

foulsham

Capital Point, 33 Bath Road, Slough, Berkshire SL1 3UF, England

Foulsham books can be found in all good bookshops and direct from
www.foulsham.com

ISBN: 978-0-572-03646-1

Copyright © 2011 G.M. Kitchen

The tax forms reproduced in this book are Crown copyright and printed with permission of HM Revenue and Customs.

The moral right of the author has been asserted.

Whilst every endeavour has been made to ensure the accuracy of the material in this book, neither the author nor the publisher can take any responsibility for any loss or problem arising.

Any suggestions for improving the information presented are always welcome and should be addressed to the author, care of the publisher, as above.

Printed in Great Britain by Thomson Litho, East Kilbride

Contents

CHAPTER ONE

Budget summary

A lthough the changes proposed in the March 2011 budget are dealt with throughout this book, this chapter summarises the main points and other relevant legislation that has occurred since the last edition was published, and gives references to the pages that deal specifically with each topic.

Personal allowances

The allowances for 2011–2012 are as follows:		Page No.
Personal allowances		
age under 65	£7,475	94
age 65–74*	£9,940	113
age 75 and over*	£10,090	113
income limit	£24,000	113

All the above personal allowances, regardless of age, will be gradually withdrawn for income over £100,000 per year at the rate of £1 of allowance lost for every £2 over £100,000 until it is completely removed.

*These allowances reduce where the income is above the income limit by £1 for every £2 of income above the limit until they reach £7,475.

(The personal allowance for people under 65 years old is to increase to £8,105 from April 2012 and the basic rate limit [see page 186] will decrease to £34,370.)

Married couple's allowance for those born before 6 April 1935		
age 75 or over	†£7,295	94
minimum amount	£2,800	94

Maintenance relief – maximum relief if born before 6 April 1935	†£2,800	90

Blind person's allowance	£1,980	95

†relief at only 10 per cent.

Individual savings accounts (ISAs)

Capital allowances

As from April 2012, the annual investment allowance for plant and machinery will reduce from £100,000 to £25,000 and the annual writing down allowance from 20 per cent to 18 per cent. The special rate writing down allowance will reduce from 10 per cent to 8 per cent and there are changes to the short life asset rules.

Capital gains tax

The capital gains tax rate for higher-rate taxpayers was increased from 18 per cent to 28 per cent from 23 June 2010. The annual exemption amount for individuals is increased from £10,100 to £10,600 from 6 April 2011. From April 2012 the consumer prices index will be used to calculate the annual exemption limit instead of the retail prices index.

Inheritance tax

The exemption threshold for 2011–2012 remains at £325,000 with the headline rate remaining at 40 per cent. These figures will be frozen until 2014–2015.

It is proposed that from April 2012, where 10 per cent or more of a net estate (after deducting exemptions, reliefs and the nil rate band) is left to charity then there will be a 10 per cent reduction in the *rate* of inheritance tax levied.

Enterpreneur's relief

The lifetime relief on gains will increase from £5m to £10m from 6 April 2011.

Enterprise investment scheme and Venture capital trusts

The rate of income tax relief under the EIS will increase from 20 per cent to 30 per cent from 6 April 2011. From April 2012 there will be increases in the qualifying thresholds for both EIS and VCT.

Page No.

Residence and domicile

The remittance basis charge option if you are not domiciled or ordinarily resident in the UK will increase from £30,000 to £50,000 per year for certain individuals from April 2012. 23

Corporation tax

The rate reduces from 28 per cent to 26 per cent for 2011–2012 and will be cut by 1 per cent in each year over the next three years reducing it to 23 per cent. The small companies rate will reduce to 20 per cent for 2011–2012. 186

Research and development

There are increases in these tax credit reliefs. 127

Penalties

From 6 April 2011, new penalties will be introduced for late filing of tax returns etc. and for late payment of tax due. 34

VAT

There are no further changes to the standard VAT rate, having increased from 17.5 per cent to 20 per cent from 4 January 2011. The VAT turnover thresholds for registration and de-registration have increased. 120

Stamp duty land tax

There is residential property stamp duty exemption on values up to £250,000 on transactions between 25 March 2010 and 25 March 2012 for first time buyers. From April 2011, there will be a new stamp duty rate of 5 per cent on properties where the proceeds of sale exceed £1m. 185

Insurance premium tax

The standard rate increased from 5 per cent to 6 per cent and the higher rate from 17.5 per cent to 20 per cent as from 4 January 2011.

Landfill tax

This tax increased to £56 per tonne from April 2011 and it will then increase further by £8 per tonne each year until 2014–2015.

CHAPTER 2

How much for you and how much for the tax inspector

A lmost everyone receives income that is liable to income tax in one form or another. You may find, however, that you can avoid paying tax, or at least reduce your tax bill, by claiming certain allowances, by offsetting various types of expense or by changing where you invest your savings.

The allowances and expenses you can claim are dealt with later in this book. This chapter tells you what income is free from tax and what income is taxable.

Taxable income can be divided into two types: earned income and unearned, or investment, income.

The tax inspector can claim part of the following types of income or benefit

Earned income

Annuities from past jobs.

Benefits – private use of firm's car, fuel, services generally.

Benefits of cheap or interest-free loans from your employer for a non-qualifying purpose (see page 72).

Bereavement allowance.

Carer's allowance.

Commission, including that from mail order companies, etc.

Compensation for loss of office (but see page 74).

Earnings from casual work and tips.

Expense allowances if not spent entirely on firm's business.

Holiday pay.

Incapacity benefit – except for the first 28 weeks.

Incentive schemes.

Income from property (but see page 86).

Income from overseas employment and pensions.

Income withdrawals from a delayed annuity pension plan.

Industrial death benefit if paid as a pension.

Invalidity pension

Jobseeker's allowance – up to the taxable maximum.

Luncheon vouchers – excess over 15p a day per person.
Maternity, paternity or adoption pay (statutory).
Pensions – from the State, previous employers or your own
    scheme.
Profits from trades or professions.
Redundancy (see page 74).
Royalties earned from your own work.
Salaries, fees and bonuses.
Sick pay (statutory).
Stipends received by the clergy.
Wages.
Widow's pension.
Widowed mother's and widowed parent's allowance.

Investment income
Annuities purchased (interest element).
Bank interest.
Building society interest and cash windfalls on a merger.
Dividends.
Gains from certain non-qualifying insurance policies.
Interest on National Savings income bonds and growth bonds.
Income from overseas investment and property.
Income from trusts and from estates of deceased persons.
National Savings interest on all savings accounts, but not the first
    £70 per person per year on ordinary accounts.
Rents and 'key' money (except holiday lettings) after expenses.
Reverse premiums.
Royalties – bought or inherited.
Stock or scrip dividends.

The following income or benefit is all yours – it is free of income tax
Adoption allowances under approved schemes.
Annuities resulting from gallantry awards.
Armed forces operational allowance (from 1 April 2006).
Attendance allowance.
Awards for damages.
Bereavement payment (lump sum).
Betting and pools winnings.
Bicycles and equipment (see page 71).
Carer income as a foster or shared lives carer.
Child benefit and allowances.
Child dependency additions paid with many State benefits.
Child tax credit.

Child trust fund income and capital gains.
Christmas bonus for pensioners from the State.
Cold weather payment.
Compensation for loss of office and redundancy pay up to £30,000 (but see page 74).
Compensation for mis-sold personal pensions and personal injury.
Council tax benefit.
Disability living allowance.
Disability or wounds pensions.
Education grants and awards from a local authority or school.
Education maintenance allowance.
Employment and support allowance.
Endowment policies.
Ex-gratia payments from your employer up to £30,000 (but see page 74).
Eye care tests and/or corrective glasses for VDU work paid by employer.
Family income supplement.
Gifts for employees provided by third parties if under £250 a year.
Gratuities from the armed forces.
Guardian's allowance.
Home improvement, repair and insulation grants.
Housing benefit and grants.
Incapacity benefit (if previously received at 12 April 1995 for the same incapacity and first 28 weeks of new claims).
Income support (unless on strike).
Individual savings account income (ISAs).
Industrial injury benefits.
Insurance policy benefits for accident, sickness, disability or unemployment.
Insurance bond withdrawals up to 5 per cent a year, but a portion may be subject to tax on redemption.
Interest on delayed tax repayments.
Interest from National Savings certificates.
Jobseeker's allowance over the taxable maximum.
Life assurance policy bonuses and profits.
Long-service awards up to £50 for each year of service (but not cash).
Lottery winnings.
Lump sums from an approved pension scheme.
Luncheon vouchers up to 15p per person per day.
Maintenance or alimony received.

Maternity and paternity allowance (statutory).
Mobile phone facilities provided by employer.
National Savings interest up to £70 per person per year on ordinary accounts only.
National and Ulster Savings certificates' increase in value.
National Savings children's bonus bonds.
New deal training allowance.
Parking facilities at or near workplace.
Pension credit.
Pensions benefits because of death or injury in the armed forces.
Pensions from Austria or Germany to victims of Nazi persecution.
Personal equity plan dividends reinvested.
Premium bond prizes.
Provident benefits up to £4,000 for lump sum payments.
Purchased life annuities – the capital proportion of yearly amount independently purchased, not as part of your pension.
Redundancy pay (statutory) (but see page 74).
Rent and council tax rebates.
Rent-a-room relief up to £4,250 a year (see page 87).
Return to work credit and in-work credit.
SAYE schemes – interest and bonus.
Severe disablement allowances.
Shares issued under an approved share incentive scheme.
Share option profits made under a SAYE scheme.
Sickness benefits under an insurance policy for up to 12 months where the premiums are paid by the employee.
Strike and unemployment pay from a trade union.
Student grants.
Subsidised or free bus travel to work.
Termination payments up to £30,000 (but see page 74).
TESSA interest if kept for the full period.
TOISA interest.
Training allowances.
Vaccine damage (lump sum).
Venture capital trust dividends (but see page 163).
War disablement pensions.
War widow or widower's pension.
Winter fuel payment.
Working tax credit.

CHAPTER 3

Tax forms and what to do with them

Tax returns

You must fill in a tax return if the tax office send you one, or you are a higher-rate taxpayer, or if you are in partnership or self-employed, or you have income to declare on which tax is due. You will also want to fill in a tax return if you have paid too much tax and are due a refund.

If you need a tax return and haven't received one, then contact the tax office that deals with your employer's PAYE or, if you are self-employed or unemployed, then contact your local tax office. There are time limits after which you will be charged penalties and interest (see page 34).

Chapter 4 takes you step by step through all aspects of the tax return and any supplementary pages. If you need supplementary tax return pages, telephone the order line on 0845 9000 404 or download them from **www.hmrc.gov.uk**.

There is also a free tax office helpline on 0845 9000 444.

Short tax return

Some taxpayers receive a 'short tax return'. As its name implies, it is much simpler and shorter than the full self assessment tax return and it is sent to those taxpayers whose tax affairs are fairly straightforward.

You must not use the short tax return if you:
- were a company director at any time in the tax year;
- received a lump sum from an employer unless it was a redundancy payment below £30,000;
- were self-employed and had more than one business; or your turnover was more than £15,000, or you changed your accounting date or want to offset losses;
- want to offset losses or pension contributions;
- were in partnership;
- are repaying a student loan;
- were involved in share options or received gains from life policies;

- received property income of more than £15,000, or had more than one property, or had furnished holiday letting income;
- received income from abroad or from a trust, etc.;
- were not resident or domiciled in the UK.

Do remember that you cannot file a short tax return electronically. If you do wish to file under this method you must request a full self assessment tax return.

There is a free tax office helpline for the short tax return on 0845 9000 444.

PAYE coding notice (form P2)

Don't just put this in a drawer and forget about it. Check it as explained on page 101.

Ensure that your employer has been notified of any alteration in your tax code by the tax office. You should write to your tax office if you disagree with any figure.

Annual earnings (form P60)

Your employer has a legal obligation to give you this form by 31 May after the end of every tax year. It shows your earnings from that employment, the total PAYE deducted in the year and total contributions made by you and your employer for national insurance.

Check the form to see if you can claim some tax back as shown in Chapter 11 (see page 103).

Income tax repayment claim (form R40)

This will be sent to you by your tax office if most of your income has had tax deducted before receipt and you normally have to claim tax back at the end of each tax year.

There is a free taxback helpline on 0845 0776 543.

Enquiry form (form 33)

This form is issued by the tax office covering your home address or a tax office that knows that you have been paid income by someone in their area. Complete and return it as soon as possible otherwise there could be delays in settling your tax matters in the future.

Notice of income paid gross (form RU6(M))

This is sometimes sent to people who have registered with banks or building societies to have their income paid gross – that is without having tax deducted.

Fill in the form carefully because the tax office send it to you to check your total income to make sure that you are not liable to pay tax (see page 116).

Notice of employee leaving (form P45)

This form is issued to you by your employer when you leave that employment. If you are immediately going to another job, hand parts 2 and 3 to your new employer. Otherwise, send them to the tax office shown on the form, together with a letter stating that you are at present unemployed, to see if you can claim a repayment of tax. Keep part 1A as you will need to refer to this when you fill in your tax return.

If you do not have this form, or if you lose it, then you will have to complete a questionnaire (form P46) obtainable from your new employer. Your employer will send this to your tax office and use a temporary PAYE code until you either provide a P45 form or the tax office advises him of a new code for you.

Return of expenses and allowances (form P11D)

This is an annual form to be completed by an employer for each employee who has received earnings, expenses and potential benefits of £8,500 or more a year. It must also be completed for all directors regardless of their earnings level. The form will detail all benefits and expenses that you were paid or given by your employer in the tax year (see Chapter 5).

There is also a form P9D for employees earning at a rate of less than £8,500 a year who have received benefits, etc. that are taxable.

Retirement enquiry form (form P161)

This form is sent to everyone who is reaching statutory retirement age and should be completed and returned to ensure that you get the correct tax allowances (see page 110).

Subcontractors in the construction industry

If you are providing services to a company involved in construction work you will normally have tax deducted from your earnings at the rate of 20 per cent before the money is paid to you. You will have received CIS25 vouchers showing the tax deducted. Send the vouchers in with your tax return. The tax return makes provision for you to declare this income, and the tax deducted, so that you are not taxed on the same amount twice. If you have established a record of regular work (and have conformed with the tax rules) for three consecutive years, then you can apply to the tax office for a CIS6 certificate that will enable you to be paid gross – there are also minimum turnover levels depending on whether you are an individual or a company. There is a helpline telephone number: 0845 366 7899.

Self assessment – tax calculation (form SA302)

This notice summarises your income tax situation and shows how much is due or has been overpaid. You must check it carefully and ensure that the figures correspond to those stated in your tax return.

As well as setting out how your tax liability (or refund) is calculated, there will quite often be comments explaining certain figures or responding to queries you have raised. It is easy to overlook these comments as the form is prepared on a computer and they don't stand out as they would in a conventional letter, therefore check the form carefully. The calculation will not reflect any payments on account you may have made and you will therefore need to check the figures with your statement of account (see below) to confirm your tax position.

If you cannot understand the calculations, or you have a query, telephone the helpline on 0845 9000 444.

If you cannot submit your tax return because you have information outstanding, you should still estimate your tax liability and make payments by the due date to avoid interest and surcharges arising on any amount unpaid. You would also avoid the late filing penalty by doing this as the penalty is restricted to the actual tax outstanding.

Self assessment – statement of account (form SA300)

This statement, sent out by your tax office, shows how much tax is due and when it should be paid; it will also show, where applicable, any payments that are due on account.

If the statement shows you have paid too much tax and the overpayment has not been refunded to you, contact your tax office to request a repayment. If you have registered to file electronically, you can access your statement at any time on the website at www.hmrc. gov.uk. One of the advantages of the self assessment tax system is that an individual now only deals with one tax office – in the past, particularly in the case of pensioners or those who have more than one employer, you could have been dealing with two or three tax offices.

Tax calculation (form P800)

This form is sent out by HMRC and shows tax owed (or overpaid) for tax years ended in 2008, 2009 and 2010.

HMRC have suffered major computer problems over the past few years and many tax returns and personal information have not been properly recorded so they have been sending out these forms with estimates of the tax they think may be under or over paid.

This is an estimate and not a final request for payment. It is important that you check it very carefully indeed. Obviously if a tax refund is due to you and you agree with the figures then send in a claim (see page 107).

If the figures are incorrect then write to your tax office advising them accordingly.

If you had previously given the tax office the correct figures and they had not acted upon them, then you can request that any arrears of tax be waived (this is known as Extra Statutory Concession A19) (see website **www.litrg.org.uk** for more information).

If you agree with the estimate of arrears of tax, you can ask for extra time to pay, or request the sum be collected under the PAYE system over, say, a two-year period if the sum is less than £2,000. (Increasing to £3,000 from April 2012.) The Government has stated that HMRC will not demand assessments under £300 per year or underpayments that have arisen due to the State pension, or other State benefits having been incorrectly attributed in their records.

General comments

You should not ignore any form or communication from the tax authorities but respond to it immediately, either by replying yourself or passing it on to the tax adviser who deals with your tax affairs.

The deadlines for returning your 2011 self assessment tax return are 31 October 2011 (or three months after the date the return form was sent to you, if later than this) or 31 January 2012 if you plan to file electronically. Interest and penalties for late submission of your tax return or tax payments are now very stringent (see page 34) and were increased in the 2011 budget.

How to fill in your 2011 tax return

Not everyone automatically receives a tax return to fill in every year, but if you do receive one, you must complete it and return it to your tax office. The tax office relies on the fact that it is the taxpayer's responsibility to advise them of any changes in sources of income or claims for expenses and allowances. You may, of course, ask for a tax return to complete if you do not receive one, by telephoning your local tax office or the tax office that deals with your PAYE if you are employed.

A husband and wife, and civil partners, are treated as individuals in their own right for tax purposes, getting their own tax return, being responsible for their own tax affairs and getting their own individual tax allowances and exemptions.

The tax year runs from 6 April in one year to 5 April in the following year.

The main tax return covers your income from savings and investments, pension income, any State benefits received and any miscellaneous income. It also covers your claim for any allowances or reliefs.

There is a separate set of pages included with your tax return called *Additional information*. You may need to complete these if:

- You have income that is not covered in the main return (such as income from Government securities, share schemes).
- You want to claim other tax reliefs (for example, married couple's allowance, maintenance payments).
- You want to claim tax losses.
- You have overseas pensions.

Don't worry about these pages immediately. Progress through the tax return as indicated in this book and you will be told if you need to use these additional information pages.

All other types of income and claims for expenses are covered in one of the eight sets of supplementary pages detailed on page TR2 of your tax return.

Read through the questions on page TR2 and tick the 'yes', 'no' and 'number' boxes as appropriate.

For clarification, these supplementary pages are summarised here with the page number in this book that deals with them in more detail. If you had more than one employer, self-employment or partnership then you need a separate set of the appropriate pages for each business.

	Page No.
Employment	
You will need these sheets if you were an employee or a director or an agency worker in the tax year, or if you received expenses payments or benefits from a former employer.	37
Self-employment	
These pages cover a situation where you work for yourself. There are two types – the short form, reproduced in this book, is for businesses that are fairly straightforward with a turnover of less than £70,000 a year, and the full version is for all other businesses.	40
Partnership	
If you were in a partnership, these are the pages you will need. As above, there are short and full versions.	43
UK property	
These pages are needed if you received income from any UK property or land.	45
Foreign	
These pages cover foreign income and gains from overseas – do not include income from employment or self-employment from overseas because that income should be declared in one of the supplementary pages referred to above.	48
Trusts etc.	
These pages cover income received from a trust, settlement or a deceased person's estate.	52

Capital gains summary

If you made capital gains, or you wish to claim an allowable capital loss, then use these pages to give the details. However, capital gains is a complicated tax and you should refer to Chapter 15 in this book to see whether you need to fill in these sheets, for not all capital gains have to be declared.

Page No. 54

Residence, remittance basis, etc.

You will need these pages if you were not resident, ordinary resident or domiciled in the UK, or you had dual residency.

57

If you have answered 'yes' to any of these questions and you do not have the appropriate supplementary pages attached to your tax return, then telephone 0845 9000 404 or fax 0845 9000 604 and request the required sheets.

Blind persons requiring Braille versions should contact their local tax office.

The main tax return

Having completed all this preparatory checking, you can now start filling in your main tax return.

Start by completing your personal details on page TR1 and then complete the student loan repayments section on page TR2 if it is applicable to you (see page 154 of this book for more details).

Student loan repayments

1 If you have received notification from the Student Loans Company that repayment of an Income Contingent Student Loan began before 6 April 2011, put 'X' in the box	2 If your employer has deducted Student Loan repayments enter the amount deducted
	£ · 0 0

Now fill in the **Income** section of the return – starting on page TR3.

UK interests, etc. and dividends

1 Taxed UK interest etc. - *the net amount after tax has been taken off (see notes)* £ · 0 0	4 Other dividends - *do not include the tax credit (see notes)* £ · 0 0
2 Untaxed UK interest etc. - *amounts which have not been taxed (see notes)* £ · 0 0	5 Foreign dividends (up to £300) - *the amount in sterling after foreign tax was taken off. Do not include this amount in the Foreign pages* £ · 0 0
3 Dividends from UK companies - *do not include the tax credit (see notes)* £ · 0 0	6 Tax taken off foreign dividends - *the sterling equivalent* £ · 0 0

You may need the following paperwork in order to summarise the figures required:

Interest statements and tax deduction certificates from UK banks, building societies and deposit takers	
Details of any National Savings investments	
Dividend vouchers	

More details regarding the information to be declared under this section can be found in Chapter 7 of this book together with some tax-saving tips. If you have investments in joint names refer to page 84.

You do not have to declare any interest in this section that is exempt from tax (for example, interest from ISAs, SAYE schemes, National Savings certificate interest, the first £70 of interest on National Savings ordinary accounts).

Although the tax office does not want you to list all of your individual dividends and interest in this tax form – you only have to state the totals – you will need to keep the details in case the tax office asks for them. Use the working sheet on page 173 of this book to keep a record.

Box 1. Show the actual amount of interest you received after tax had been deducted. Include the interest element of purchased life annuities here, but exclude the capital element (see page 117).

Box 2. Show the total interest you received that did not have any tax deducted.

Box 3. This is for dividends from UK companies, excluding the tax credit.

Box 4. This is for dividends from authorised unit trusts and open-ended investment companies, etc. – show the amounts actually received, excluding the tax credit.

Box 5. If you have any dividends from overseas you can enter the gross amount here if the total is less than £300; (if it is more, then you will have to complete the Foreign supplementary pages (see page 48).

Box 6. Any tax deducted from foreign dividends should be shown here.

Do not include interest from Government stocks (gilt-edged securities) in this section – this needs to be declared in the *Additional information* supplementary pages (see page 60).

UK pensions, annuities and other State benefits received

7 State Pension - *the amount due for the year (see notes)*	11 Tax taken off box 10
£ · 0 0	£ · 0 0
8 State Pension lump sum	12 Taxable Incapacity Benefit and contribution-based Employment and Support Allowance - *see notes*
£ · 0 0	£ · 0 0
9 Tax taken off box 8	13 Tax taken off Incapacity Benefit in box 12
£ · 0 0	£ · 0 0
10 Pensions (other than State Pension), retirement annuities and taxable triviality payments - *give details of the payers, amounts paid and tax deducted in the 'Any other information' box, box 19, on page TR 6*	14 Jobseeker's Allowance
	£ · 0 0
£ · 0 0	15 Total of any other taxable State Pensions and benefits
	£ · 0 0

You may need the following paperwork to summarise the figures required:

Your annual State pension letter or statements	
A P60 form or certificate of tax deducted in the case of any other pension	
Benefit office or DWP statements in respect of any incapacity benefit or other taxable State benefit or jobseeker's allowance	

More information and tax tips on the figures to go in this section can be found in Chapter 7 on page 83.

Box 7. This is not just for the basic State pension – you need to include any additional or graduated State pension. Do not include the State Christmas bonus or winter fuel payment as they are not taxable. A married woman should enter in her own tax return any pension she receives even if it is paid as a result of her husband's contributions.

Box 8. If you have deferred taking the State pension and have now received a lump sum payment, show the amount here.

Box 9. Note any tax deducted.

Box 10. All other pensions you receive should be added together (before any tax deducted) and entered here.

Enter the details of pensions and annuities in box 20, as this will help the tax office in deducting the correct amount of tax. Some UK pensions for service to an overseas government have a 10 per cent exemption from UK tax, in which case only 90 per cent of the pension needs to be declared – clearly state this on the form.

Use the working sheet on page 178 of this book to collate the various pension amounts. Remember that pensions received from abroad should be entered in the Foreign supplementary pages of your tax return, not in this section.

Box 11. Enter the tax deducted.

Box 12. Only incapacity benefit and contribution-based Employment and Support Allowances received after the first 28 weeks is taxable and needs to be entered. Benefit that commenced before 13 April 2005 is not taxable.

Box 13. Enter the amount of any tax deducted.

Box 14. Enter the taxable amount of jobseeker's allowance.

Box 15. Any other taxable State pensions or benefits received that are not covered in the earlier boxes should be entered here. See page 78.

Other UK income not included on supplementary pages

Do not use this section for income that should be returned on supplementary pages. Share schemes, gilts, stock dividends, life insurance gains and certain other kinds of income go on the *Additional information* pages in the tax return pack.

16 Other taxable income - *before expenses and tax taken off*

£ ☐☐☐☐☐☐☐ . 0 0

17 Total amount of allowable expenses - *read page TRG 14 of the tax return guide*

£ ☐☐☐☐☐☐☐ . 0 0

18 Any tax taken off box 16

£ ☐☐☐☐☐☐☐ . 0 0

19 Benefit from pre-owned assets - *read page TRG 15 of the guide*

£ ☐☐☐☐☐☐☐ . 0 0

20 Description of income in boxes 16 and 19 - *if there is not enough space here please give details in the 'Any other information' box, box 19, on page TR 6*

This section basically covers any other type of income that has not been declared above, or is not covered by the supplementary pages, which you would have ticked on the check list on page TR2 of the tax return.

Box 16. This is particularly useful for declaring any miscellaneous income from casual work, insurance or mail order commission, royalties, freelance income etc. Use the working sheets at the back of this book to add together the various types of income – it is only the total that needs to be entered in the return. Rather surprisingly, box 16 also covers here any dividends or distributions from real estate investment trusts (REITs).

Box 17. This gives you the opportunity of claiming any expenses against any of the income declared in box 16. See Chapter 6 for guidance as to what you can claim and any tax tips. Collate your expenses in the working sheets on page 176, as the tax office may ask for more specific details at a later date, and put the total in this box.

Box 18. If any tax had been deducted before you received any income, show the total tax here.

Box 19. Benefits from pre-owned assets arises from the inheritance legislation and is now incorporated in this section of the tax return and any such benefits need to be declared in box 19. This subject is dealt with on page 145 of this book. Your calculation as to how you arrive at this figure needs to be shown in box 20.

Box 20. This enables you state the broad details of the income declared in boxes 16 and 19 – you just need to state from where the income arose, for example, 'royalties £251'.

The tax return now covers reliefs and allowances that you can claim as a deduction from your income.

Pension contributions

Paying into registered pension schemes and overseas pension schemes

Do not include payments you make to your employer's pension scheme which are deducted from your pay before tax or payments made by your employer.

1 Payments to registered pension schemes where basic rate tax relief will be claimed by your pension provider (called 'relief at source'). Enter the payments and basic rate tax

£ ⬜⬜⬜⬜⬜⬜⬜ · 0 0

2 Payments to a retirement annuity contract where basic rate tax relief will not be claimed by your provider

£ ⬜⬜⬜⬜⬜⬜⬜ · 0 0

3 Payments to your employer's scheme which were not deducted from your pay before tax

£ ⬜⬜⬜⬜⬜⬜⬜ · 0 0

4 Payments to an overseas pension scheme which is not UK-registered which are eligible for tax relief and were not deducted from your pay before tax

£ ⬜⬜⬜⬜⬜⬜⬜ · 0 0

You may need the following paperwork to find the figures required:

Pension statements from the insurance company or from the trustees of your employer's scheme	

More information and tax advice on pensions and pension contributions can be found on pages 163–167 of this book, which also covers any pension savings tax charges and other liabilities that will need to be declared in another part of the tax return.

Most contributions to an employer's pension scheme are deducted from an employees pay and the employee is therefore getting tax relief automatically. You do not have to enter these contributions in the tax return.

Box 1. This covers payments you have made directly to a pension provider. These will have been made net of basic rate tax and you need to add this tax to the net amount you have actually paid to arrive at the figure to declare in your tax return. If you are entitled to higher rate tax relief then this will be adjusted in your end of year tax calculation.

Box 2. This covers any authorised payment you have made to a retirement annuity contract which will not have had basic rate tax deducted from the payments. Show the amount you have actually paid.

Box 3. If for any reason your employer was unable to deduct basic rate tax from your pension contribution then enter the amount contributed in box 3. Tax relief will be calculated and shown on your end of year tax calculation.

Box 4. You may be in a position where you make contributions to an overseas pension scheme, in which case basic rate tax will not have been deducted. Show the amount contributed in this box.

Charitable giving

5	Gift Aid payments made in the year to 5 April 2011		9	Value of qualifying shares or securities gifted to charity
	£ ⬜⬜⬜⬜⬜⬜⬜⬜ · 0 0			£ ⬜⬜⬜⬜⬜⬜⬜⬜ · 0 0
6	Total of any 'one-off' payments in box 5		10	Value of qualifying land and buildings gifted to charity
	£ ⬜⬜⬜⬜⬜⬜⬜⬜ · 0 0			£ ⬜⬜⬜⬜⬜⬜⬜⬜ · 0 0
7	Gift Aid payments made in the year to 5 April 2011 but treated as if made in the year to 5 April 2010		11	Value of qualifying investments gifted to non-UK charities in boxes 9 and 10
	£ ⬜⬜⬜⬜⬜⬜⬜⬜ · 0 0			£ ⬜⬜⬜⬜⬜⬜⬜⬜ · 0 0
8	Gift Aid payments made after 5 April 2011 but to be treated as if made in the year to 5 April 2011		12	Gift Aid payments to non-UK charities in box 5
	£ ⬜⬜⬜⬜⬜⬜⬜⬜ · 0 0			£ ⬜⬜⬜⬜⬜⬜⬜⬜ · 0 0

You may need the following in order to find the figures required:

Copies of any signed covenants	
Records of cash donations	
Contract notes for shares, assets, etc.	
Certificates from charities confirming gifts	

You do not have to enter any sums contributed under a payroll giving scheme as you will have already received tax relief because your employer will have deducted your contribution from your pay before applying PAYE tax.

Box 5. This refers to *regular* gift aid payments – use the working sheet on page 179 of this book to keep a record of how you arrive at the total to go in your tax return. Enter the amounts actually paid by you. If you have previously asked that any tax repayment due to you should, instead, be paid to a charity, then you should include this amount in the total.

Box 6. This covers incidental gift aid payments that you may not necessarily repeat on a regular basis.

Box 7. If you had stated in your last tax return that you wanted payments made in the 2010–2011 tax year applied to your previous years' earning, state the amount in box 7. (See also page 91.)

Box 8. Conversely, if you think it would be beneficial to you tax-wise to have any such payments made between 6 April 2011 and the date you send in your tax return applied to the 2010–2011 year, then enter such sum in box 8.

Boxes 9 and 10. The above boxes dealt with any cash payments you made to charity. You may have gifted shares or land or buildings, in which case enter the amounts here.

Boxes 11 and 12. Include gifts made to non-UK charities here.

Tips on tax-efficient ways of giving to charity are on page 91.

Blind person's allowance

13	If you are registered blind on a local authority or other register, put 'X' in the box	15	If you want your spouse's, or civil partner's, surplus allowance, put 'X' in the box
	☐		☐
14	Enter the name of the local authority or other register	16	If you want your spouse, or civil partner, to have your surplus allowance, put 'X' in the box
	☐		☐

Boxes 13 and 14. You can claim for the blind person's allowance by completing these boxes. Not all local authorities in Scotland and Northern Ireland maintain a register of blind persons. Provided you meet all the qualifications for the allowance, you should enter either 'Scottish claim' or 'Northern Ireland claim' in this section.

Boxes 15 and 16. If it is beneficial to transfer this allowance between partners, then put an 'X' in either of these boxes (see Chapter 9 for help here).

Service companies

1	If you provided your services through a service company (a company which provides your personal services to third parties), enter the total of the dividends (including the tax credit) and salary (before tax was taken off) you withdrew from the company in the tax year – *read page TRG 21 of the guide*
	£ ▢▢▢▢▢▢▢▢▢ · 0 0

You have to state here any income declared in your tax return that originated from a service company. Do not complete this box if *all* the income from the company was employment income as distinct from dividends. This is still a very grey area of the tax legislation and is covered on page 129 of this book.

Finishing your tax return

You will not have finished your tax return until you have completed any supplementary pages – refresh your memory by checking the summary on pages 22–23 of this book.

Do you want to calculate your own tax? If you do, you can either use the tax calculation summary pages that the tax office can supply (telephone 0845 9000 404 if you want a copy or download from **www. hmrc.gov.uk**), which are very comprehensive as they have to cover all conceivable situations and are thus necessarily complicated; or you can use the *Check Your Tax* calculator on page 170 of this book if your tax affairs are fairly straightforward.

Tax refunded or set-off

1	If you have had any 2010-11 Income Tax refunded or set off by us or Jobcentre Plus, enter the amount
	£ . 0 0

State the amount in box 1 if you have received any tax refunded in respect of the 2010–2011 tax year.

If you have not paid enough tax

2	If you owe tax for 2010-11 and have a PAYE tax code, we will try to collect the tax due (if less than £2,000) through your tax code for 2012-13, unless you put 'X' in the box – *read page TRG 22 of the guide*	3	If you are likely to owe tax for **2011–12** on income other than employed earnings or pensions, and you do **not** want us to use your 2011-12 PAYE tax code to collect that tax during the year, put 'X' in the box – *read page TRG 22 of the guide*
	☐		☐

Box 2. Any underpayment of tax below £2,000 for 2010–2011 will normally be collected by an adjustment in your PAYE tax if the return is submitted by the 31 October 2011 deadline unless you put an 'X' in box 2, in which case you will have to send a cheque to HMRC when the liability is agreed.

Box 3. If it is likely that you will owe tax for 2011–2012 and you don't want the tax office to make an allowance for this in your next PAYE code number (for example, you may not want your employer to know of the existence of other earnings) then put an 'X' in box 3.

If you have paid too much tax or you have a tax adviser

4	Name of bank or building society	10	If you have entered a nominee's name in box 5, put 'X' in the box
			☐
5	Name of account holder (or nominee)	11	If your nominee is your tax adviser, put 'X' in the box
			☐
		12	Nominee's address
6	Branch sort code		
	☐☐ – ☐☐ – ☐☐		
7	Account number	13	and postcode
8	Building society reference number	14	To authorise your nominee to receive any repayment, you must sign in the box. A photocopy of your signature will not do
9	If you do not have a bank or building society account, or if you want us to send a cheque to you or to your nominee, put 'X' in the box		
	☐		

| 15 | Your tax adviser's name | | 17 | The first line of their address and the postcode |

| 16 | Their phone number | | 18 | The reference your adviser uses for you |

Any other information

| 19 | Please give any other information in this space |

Boxes 4 to 18. Fill in all your personal bank details so that any refund can be paid directly into your bank account; similarly fill in the requested details if you have a tax adviser. See page 92 if you want to donate your refund to a charity.

Box 19. Use this if you want to bring to the notice of the tax office any major change in your tax affairs.

Signing your form and sending it back
Box 20. If some of the figures in your tax return are estimated, put an 'X' here. Wherever possible it is better to provide accurate figures when you send in your return as this will prevent you having to correspond, perhaps extensively, with the tax office and may delay agreeing your tax liability, which may result in penalties and interest.

Box 21. Put an 'X' here if you are enclosing any supplementary pages (see page 22).

| 20 | If this tax return contains provisional or estimated figures, put 'X' in the box | 21 | If you are enclosing separate supplementary pages, put 'X' in the box |

| 22 | If you give false information, you may have to pay financial penalties and face prosecution. Please sign and date this form. |

The information I have given on this tax return and any supplementary pages is correct and complete to the best of my knowledge and belief

Date DD MM YYYY

Signature

| 23 | If you have signed on behalf of someone else, enter the capacity. For example, executor, receiver | 25 | If you filled in boxes 23 and 24 enter your name |

| 24 | Enter the name of the person you have signed for | 26 | and your address |

Boxes 22 to 26. Make sure that you sign and date the declaration. A surprising number of returns are unsigned and the tax office will return them – if you are close to the filing deadline this omission could render your return 'late' and you may have to pay penalties.

When you sign your tax return, you are declaring that to the best of your knowledge the return is complete, true and accurate.

It is often thought that if you keep quiet about some of your income, then the tax inspector will not find out about it. This is not the case. The tax authorities have many sources of information, the most common being your employer, banks, building societies and other businesses, all of whom may be required to make a declaration of payments made to individuals and businesses.

What if you have made a mistake?

Do not worry if you have forgotten to claim an allowance due to you, for you have a time limit of four years from the end of the tax year to which it applies in which to tell your tax office of your mistake and claim a refund.

If you forget to include some of your income on the form, you should immediately notify your tax office explaining your error.

When to send in your 2011 tax return

You must send in your tax return by 31 October 2011, or if you received the form after 31 July, then three months from the date of receipt. You have until 31 January 2012 if you file your form electronically via the internet – see below.

Where to pay

The address to which you have to send your payment is stated on the HMRC paperwork. If you are paying by post, the Shipley accounts office address is HMRC Accounts Office, Bradford BD98 1YY. The Cumbernauld postal address is HMRC Accounts Office, Bradford BD98 1GG.

The HMRC bank sort code is 08 32 10. The account number is 12011020 for Shipley payments, and 12001039 for Cumbernauld payments.

Payments on account

If you have several sources of untaxed income or you are self-employed, it is likely that you will have to make two payments on account for each tax year. For example, for the year ended 5 April 2011 the first payment of 50 per cent of your anticipated tax bill should have been made by 31 January 2011 and the second 50 per cent on 31 July 2011;

any balance due, once your tax liability is agreed, is payable on 31 January 2012, although a refund may be dealt with as soon as agreed.

It is up to you to work out how much you need to pay on account. If you believe your income will be lower than the year for which your payments on account have been calculated and you wish to alter the figure that the tax office has demanded, then ask for form SA303 on which you can explain your reasons. If your claim to reduce the tax due is excessive and you have a liability at the end of the tax year, then interest will be payable from the original date the payments should have been made on these excess reductions.

Penalties and fines

Higher penalties have been introduced from April 2011 for late filing of tax returns and late payment of any tax due, as detailed below. There also fines for failure to keep adequate records to support figures in your tax return, and for not declaring taxable income, etc.

Penalties for filing late

There will be an automatic penalty of £100 if your 2011 tax return is sent in late, and if it is three months late then an additional penalty of £10 per day will be levied, up to a maximum of £900. If you are six months late there will be a further penalty of 5 per cent of tax due or £300 whichever is the greater, and at 12 months late another 5 per cent or £300. In serious cases HMRC can levy higher penalties.

Penalties for paying late

In addition to the above, you will have to pay interest of 5 per cent on any unpaid tax if you are 30 days late, a further 5 per cent at six months late and another 5 per cent at 12 months late.

Filing your tax return over the internet

You can file your full tax return (but not the short version) and the supplementary pages over the internet if you find that is more convenient.

Go to **www.hmrc.gov.uk** to download the free HMRC software package.

Alternatively you can use one of the many commercial software packages available, which are listed on the HMRC website. You can telephone your tax office on the number shown on your tax return; if not, you can ring the helpline 0845 9000 444 if you have any problems.

What paperwork will you need?

To save time whilst you are online, make sure you have to hand all the paperwork to which you may need to refer. You may need forms P60, P11D or P45 unless you are self-employed, in which case you will need your detailed accounts. Additionally you may need statements covering any interest, dividends or rents received as well as details of any pension income, benefits and casual earnings summaries. If you are going to declare capital gains or losses, then you will need full details and history of all your transactions.

The benefits of filing electronically

The main advantages are:

- You have an extended time frame in which to file your return – until 31 January 2012 instead of 31 October 2011.
- The tax calculation is automatically done on the computer but do check it carefully before submitting in case you have typed in £5,000 of interest received instead of £500, for example.
- You get an immediate acknowledgement of filing, and repayments are faster.
- The service is safe, secure, available 24 hours a day and you can view your statement (SA300) at any time.

How to register

To register, log on to **www.hmrc.gov.uk**.

You will need your tax reference number or national insurance number. Once you have registered you will have to wait about seven days to receive confirmation in the post of your ID and a separate unique activation PIN number. Once you have this, plus a password selected by you, you can log in and start filing. As a security precaution, don't forget to destroy the communication giving you your PIN number.

Remember to print out a hard copy of your completed tax return so you can refer to it later.

Problems with your tax office

Contact your tax enquiry office initially if you have a query; then your tax inspector. If you still do not get satisfaction, ask for a different complaints handler to review the case. If your query is still not resolved satisfactorily, you can contact the adjudicator's office (see **www.adjudicatorsoffice.gov.uk**).

Keep your records

The law requires you to keep all records of earnings, income, benefits, profits and expenses, etc. and all relevant information, including copies of emails, for 22 months from the end of the tax year and five years and ten months if you are self-employed.

If the tax office have commenced a formal enquiry into a tax return before the expiry of the time limit, the records must be kept until that enquiry is completed.

Supplementary pages

Having completed the main tax return, you now have to complete any supplementary pages that you ticked as 'yes' on page TR2 of your tax return.

Employment

The supplementary pages headed *Employment* cover your income and benefits from employment and your claim for expenses. (There are different versions of this form for ministers of religion and Members of Parliament and the regional assemblies.)

After each section there is a cross-reference to the chapter or page in this book that will give you help in filling in this form.

To fill in these sections you may need copies of your:

P60 or P45 forms	
Notice of tax code	
P11D form	
Receipts for expenses, etc.	

HM Revenue & Customs

Employment

Tax year 6 April 2010 to 5 April 2011

Your name

Your Unique Taxpayer Reference (UTR)

Complete an *Employment* page for each employment or directorship

1 Pay from this employment - the total from your P45 or P60 - *before tax was taken off*

£ . 0 0

2 UK tax taken off pay in box 1

£ . 0 0

3 Tips and other payments not on your P60 - *read page EN 3 of the notes*

£ . 0 0

4 PAYE tax reference of your employer (on your P45/P60)

/

5 Your employer's name

6 If you were a company director, put 'X' in the box

7 And, if the company was a close company, put 'X' in the box

8 If you are a part-time teacher in England or Wales and are on the Repayment of Teachers' Loans Scheme for this employment, put 'X' in the box

---

Pay from your employer and employment details

Refer to Chapter 5 (see page 67) for more background information and advice on employment income and benefits.

Boxes 1 and 2. You will find the totals to go in these boxes on the P60 form your employer will have given you at the year end (see page 67); if you have left an employment, you will need to get the figure from the P45 form that you received from your previous employer.

Any deductions made by your employer for your contributions to an approved pension scheme, payroll giving donations, or taxable lump sum leaving payment should have been deducted from the figure shown on your P60 form and only this net earnings figure should be shown in box 1 but before deducting any tax.

You do not have to include in the tax return any child tax credit or working tax credit that you may have received.

Any jobseeker's allowance included in your P60 or P45 form should not be shown here but in box 14 on page TR3 of your main tax return (see page 25).

Box 3. Tips and gratuities should be shown here if they are not included in your P60 form.

Boxes 4 to 8. Fill in the personal details.

Benefits from your employment

9 Company cars and vans - *the total 'cash equivalent' amount*	**13** Goods and other assets provided by your employer *- the total value or amount*
£ · 0 0	£ · 0 0
10 Fuel for company cars and vans - *the total 'cash equivalent' amount*	**14** Accommodation provided by your employer - *the total value or amount*
£ · 0 0	£ · 0 0
11 Private medical and dental insurance - *the total 'cash equivalent' amount*	**15** Other benefits (including interest-free and low interest loans) - *the total 'cash equivalent' amount*
£ · 0 0	£ · 0 0
12 Vouchers, credit cards and excess mileage allowance	**16** Expenses payments received and balancing charges
£ · 0 0	£ · 0 0

Boxes 9 and 10. Company cars and vans see pages 68 and 71.

    Box 11. See page 72.

    Box 12. See page 72.

    Box 13. See page 73.

    Box 14. See page 72.

    Box 15. See pages 72–74.

    Box 16. See pages 73 and 126.

Note that share option schemes and share benefits and lump sum compensation paid on termination of employment have to be declared on the *Additional information pages* (see page 62).

Employment expenses

Employment expenses		
17 Business travel and subsistence expenses		**19** Professional fees and subscriptions
£ ⸱ 0 0		£ ⸱ 0 0
18 Fixed deductions for expenses		**20** Other expenses and capital allowances
£ ⸱ 0 0		£ ⸱ 0 0

Boxes 17 to 20. These allow you to claim authorised expenses which you can set against your income for tax purposes. These are fully covered, with tax advice, in Chapter 6 (see page 80). Use the working sheets at the back of this book to add together the various expenses, as you only have to put the total in the tax return. The tax office may ask for details at a later date.

More than one employment

All the boxes on page E1 are repeated on page E2 in case you have, or have had, a second employment during the tax year, for you must declare income and expenses from each employment separately; you may need further copies of these sheets if you have more than two employers (for example, you are a director of several companies). Telephone 0845 9000 404 if you require further copies.

Self-employment

These supplementary pages cover your business details. There are two types of supplementary pages ('short' and 'full'). The short version reproduced here can be used where your turnover is less than £70,000 a year (or pro-rata if you have not been trading for a full year). A separate sheet needs to be completed for each business. There is a different version for Lloyds underwriting names.

To fill in these sections you may need copies of:

Financial accounts and records	
Previous year's tax records	
Details of capital expenditure	

You must fill in these pages if you were in business on a self-employed or freelance basis, or you let furnished rooms and provided services so that it was considered as a business. If you were in partnership, you need the *Partnership* supplementary pages (see page 43). See page 27 if your freelance earnings could be considered as casual and not ongoing.

Although these supplementary pages appear very complicated at first glance, they are basically requesting the information that should be available from your business accounts but they are summarised under individual boxes for turnover and expense headings, with separate boxes for capital allowances, adjustments to profits for tax purposes and carrying forward of any losses.

Chapter 13 (see page 119) covers all basic aspects of self-employment, including those expenses that are not allowed for tax as well as deductions that you can make.

HM Revenue & Customs

Self-employment (short)
Tax year 6 April 2010 to 5 April 2011

Your name

Your Unique Taxpayer Reference (UTR)

Read page SESN 1 of the *notes* to check if you should use this page or the *Self-employment (full)* page.

Business details

1 Description of business

2 Postcode of your business address

3 If your business name, description, address or postcode have changed in the last 12 months, put 'X' in the box and give details in the 'Any other information' box of your tax return

4 If you are a foster carer or shared lives carer, put 'X' in the box – *read page SESN 2 of the notes*

5 If your business started after 5 April 2010, enter the start date *DD MM YYYY*

6 If your business ceased before 6 April 2011, enter the final date of trading

7 Date your books or accounts are made up to – *read page SESN 3 of the notes*

Business income – if your annual business turnover was below £70,000

8 Your turnover – *the takings, fees, sales or money earned by your business*
£

9 Any other business income not included in box 8 – *excluding Business Start-up Allowance*
£

Allowable business expenses

If your annual turnover was below £70,000 you may just put your total expenses in box 19, rather than filling in the whole section.

10 Costs of goods bought for resale or goods used
£

11 Car, van and travel expenses – *after private use proportion*
£

12 Wages, salaries and other staff costs
£

13 Rent, rates, power and insurance costs
£

14 Repairs and renewals of property and equipment
£

15 Accountancy, legal and other professional fees
£

16 Interest and bank and credit card etc. financial charges
£

17 Phone, fax, stationery and other office costs
£

18 Other allowable business expenses – *client entertaining costs are not an allowable expense*
£

19 Total allowable expenses – *total of boxes 10 to 18*
£

Net profit or loss

20 Net profit – *if your business income is more than your expenses (if box 8 + box 9 minus box 19 is positive)*

£ [   ] . 0 0

21 Or, net loss – *if your expenses exceed your business income (if box 19 minus (box 8 + box 9) is positive)*

£ [   ] . 0 0

Tax allowances for vehicles and equipment (capital allowances)

There are 'capital' tax allowances for vehicles and equipment used in your business (you should not have included the cost of these in your business expenses). Read pages SESN 4 to SESN 8 of the *notes* and use the example and Working Sheets to work out your capital allowances.

22 Annual Investment Allowance

£ [   ] . 0 0

24 Other capital allowances

£ [   ] . 0 0

23 Allowance for small balance of unrelieved expenditure

£ [   ] . 0 0

25 Total balancing charges – where you have disposed of items for more than their value

£ [   ] . 0 0

Boxes 22 to 25. Refer to pages 125 and 126.

Calculating your taxable profits

Your taxable profit may not be the same as your net profit. Read page SESN 9 of the *notes* to see if you need to make any adjustments and fill in the boxes which apply to arrive at your taxable profit for the year.

26 Goods and/or services for your own use – *read page SESN 8 of the notes*

£ [   ] . 0 0

28 Loss brought forward from earlier years set off against this year's profits – *up to the amount in box 27*

£ [   ] . 0 0

27 Net business profit for tax purposes (if box 20 + box 25 + box 26 minus (boxes 21 to 24) is positive)

£ [   ] . 0 0

29 Any other business income not included in boxes 8 or 9 – *for example, Business Start-up Allowance*

£ [   ] . 0 0

Total taxable profits or net business loss

30 Total taxable profits from this business (if box 27 + box 29 minus box 28 is positive)

£ [   ] . 0 0

31 Net business loss for tax purposes (if boxes 21 to 24 *minus* (box 20 + box 25 + box 26) is positive)

£ [   ] . 0 0

Losses, Class 4 NICs and CIS deductions

If you have made a loss for tax purposes (box 31), read page SESN 9 of the *notes* and fill in boxes 32 to 34 as appropriate.

32 Loss from this tax year set off against other income for 2010–11

£ [   ] . 0 0

35 If you are exempt from paying Class 4 NICs, put 'X' in the box – *read page SESN 10 of the notes*

[ ]

33 Loss to be carried back to previous year(s) and set off against income (or capital gains)

£ [   ] . 0 0

36 If you have been given a 2010–11 Class 4 NICs deferment certificate, put 'X' in the box – *read page SESN 10 of the notes*

[ ]

34 Total loss to carry forward after all other set-offs – *including unused losses brought forward*

£ [   ] . 0 0

37 Deductions on payment and deduction statements from contractors – *construction industry subcontractors only*

£ [   ] . 0 0

Partnership

All the background information needed to complete these pages is similar to that covered by the Self-employment section (see page 40) and Chapter 13 (see page 119) covers most of the basic aspects.

To fill in these sections you may need copies of:

Partnership statements and accounts	
Previous tax records	
Details of capital expenditure	

There are two types of supplementary pages: *Partnership* (short version) reproduced here and *Partnership* (full version). Use the short version if your only partnership income was trading income or taxed interest from banks, building societies or deposit takers. This will apply to the majority of small partnerships.

HM Revenue & Customs

Partnership (short)

Tax year 6 April 2010 to 5 April 2011

Your name

Your Unique Taxpayer Reference (UTR)

Complete a *Partnership* page for each partnership of which you were a member and for each business

Partnership details

1 Partnership reference number

2 Description of partnership trade or profession

3 If you became a partner after 5 April 2010, enter the date you joined the partnership *DD MM YYYY*

4 If you left the partnership after 5 April 2010 and before 6 April 2011, enter the date you left

Your share of the partnership's trading or professional profits

If you need help, look up the box numbers in the *notes*. If you want to enter a loss, or an adjustment needs to be taken off, put a minus sign (-) in the box next to the £ sign.

5 Date your basis period began

6 Date your basis period ended

7 Your share of the partnership's profit or loss – *from box 11 or 12 on the Partnership Statement*

12 Overlap relief used this year

13 Overlap profit carried forward

14 Adjusted profit for 2010-11 – *see the Working Sheet on page SPN 5 of the notes*

8 If your basis period is not the same as the partnership's accounting period, enter the adjustment needed to arrive at the profit or loss for your basis period

£ _____ . 0 0

9 Adjustment for change of accounting practice - *from box 11A on the Partnership Statement*

£ _____ . 0 0

10 Averaging adjustment - *only for farmers, market gardeners and creators of literary or artistic works*

£ _____ . 0 0

11 Foreign tax claimed as a deduction - *only if Foreign Tax Credit Relief has not been claimed on Foreign pages*

£ _____ . 0 0

15 Losses brought forward from earlier years set off against this year's profit (up to the amount in box 14)

£ _____ . 0 0

16 Taxable profits after losses brought forward (box 14 minus box 15)

£ _____ . 0 0

17 Any other business income not included in the partnership accounts

£ _____ . 0 0

18 Your share of total taxable profits from the partnership's business for 2010-11 (box 16 + box 17)

£ _____ . 0 0

Your share of the partnership's trading or professional losses

19 Adjusted loss for 2010-11 - *see the Working Sheet on page SPN 5 of the notes*

£ _____ . 0 0

20 Loss from this tax year set off against other income for 2010-11

£ _____ . 0 0

21 Loss to be carried back to previous year(s) and set off against income (or capital gains)

£ _____ . 0 0

22 Total loss to carry forward after all other set-offs - *including unused losses brought forward*

£ _____ . 0 0

Class 4 National Insurance contributions (NICs)

23 If you are exempt from paying Class 4 NICs, put 'X' in the box - *read page SPN 6 of the notes*

24 If you have been given a 2010-11 Class 4 NICs deferment certificate, put 'X' in the box - *read page SPN 6 of the notes*

25 Adjustment to profits chargeable to Class 4 NICs - *read page SPN 7 of the notes*

£ _____ . 0 0

Your share of the partnership taxed interest etc.

26 Your share of taxed interest etc. - *from box 22 on the Partnership Statement*

£ _____ . 0 0

Your share of the partnership tax paid and deductions

27 Your share of Income Tax taken off partnership income - *from box 25 on the Partnership Statement*

£ _____ . 0 0

28 Your share of CIS deductions made by contractors - *from box 24 on the Partnership Statement*

£ _____ . 0 0

29 Your share of any tax taken off trading income (not contractor deductions) - *from box 24A on the Partnership Statement*

£ _____ . 0 0

Any other information

30 Please give any other information in this space

UK property

The supplementary pages headed UK property cover all types of UK rental income, whether it is from numerous properties or a single rental, holiday lettings, or qualifies for rent-a-room relief. Income from letting furnished accommodation in the EEA can also be included here.

Any other income from land or property overseas should not be included here but in the Foreign supplementary pages and if you are running a business or trade (such as a guest house), use the *Self-employed* supplementary pages.

Page 86 of this book gives you background details regarding the taxation of land and property, joint holdings and expenses payments you might be able to claim.

Box 4. If you are only claiming rent-a-room relief for gross rents of £4,250 or less a year put a cross in box 4 and/or fill in box 35 (see page 87).

To fill in these pages of the tax return you may need:

Records of rent received	
Records of expenses and invoices for the property	

HM Revenue & Customs

UK property

Tax year 6 April 2010 to 5 April 2011

Your name

Your Unique Taxpayer Reference (UTR)

UK property details

1 Number of properties rented out

2 If all property income ceased in 2010-11 and you do not expect to receive such income in 2011-12, put 'X' in the box

3 If you have any income from property let jointly, put 'X' in the box

4 If you are claiming Rent a Room relief and your rents are £4,250 or less (or £2,125 if let jointly), put 'X' in the box

Furnished holiday lettings in the UK or EEA

Please read pages UKPN 2 to 5 of the *notes* if you have furnished holiday lettings

5 Income – *the amount of rent and any income for services provided to tenants*

£ _____ · 0 0

6 Rent paid, repairs, insurance and costs of services provided – *the total amount*

£ _____ · 0 0

7 Loan interest and other financial costs

£ _____ · 0 0

8 Legal, management and other professional fees

£ _____ · 0 0

9 Other allowable property expenses

£ _____ · 0 0

10 Private use adjustment – *if expenses include any amounts for non-business purposes*

£ _____ · 0 0

11 Balancing charges – *read page UKPN 5 of the notes*

£ _____ · 0 0

12 Capital allowances – *read page UKPN 5 of the notes*

£ _____ · 0 0

13 Profit for the year (if the amount in box 5 + box 10 + box 11 minus (boxes 6 to 9 + box 12) is positive)

£ _____ · 0 0

Furnished holiday lettings losses

Please read pages UKPN 5 and 6 of the *notes* before filling in boxes 14 to 17

14 Loss for the year (if boxes 6 to 9 + box 12 minus (box 5 + box 10 + box 11) is positive)

£ _____ · 0 0

15 Loss set off against other income from property

£ _____ · 0 0

16 Loss set off against 2010-11 total income

£ _____ · 0 0

17 Loss carried back to earlier years

£ _____ · 0 0

Property income

Do not include Real Estate Investment Trust or Property Authorised Investment Funds dividends/distributions here

18 Total rents and other income from property (including any furnished holiday lettings profits in box 13)

£ _____ · 0 0

19 Tax taken off any income in box 18

£ _____ · 0 0

20 Premiums for the grant of a lease – *from box E on the Working Sheet on page UKPN 7 of the notes.*

£ _____ · 0 0

21 Reverse premiums and inducements

£ _____ · 0 0

Property expenses

22 Rent, rates, insurance, ground rents etc.

£ _____ · 0 0

23 Property repairs, maintenance and renewals

£ _____ · 0 0

24 Loan interest and other financial costs

£ _____ · 0 0

25 Legal, management and other professional fees

£ _____ · 0 0

26 Costs of services provided, including wages

£ _____ · 0 0

27 Other allowable property expenses

£ _____ · 0 0

Calculating your taxable profit or loss

28 Private use adjustment – *read page UKPN 9 of the notes*

£ _____ · 0 0

29 Balancing charges – *read page UKPN 9 of the notes*

£ _____ · 0 0

30 Annual Investment Allowance

£ _____ · 0 0

31 Business Premises Renovation Allowance (Assisted Areas only) – *read page UKPN 10 of the notes*

£ _____ · 0 0

32 All other capital allowances

£ _____ · 0 0

33 Landlord's Energy Saving Allowance

£ _____ · 0 0

34 10% wear and tear allowance – *for furnished residential accommodation only*

£ _____ · 0 0

35 Rent a Room exempt amount

£ _____ · 0 0

36 Adjusted profit for the year – *from box O on the Working Sheet on page UKPN 14*

£ _____ · 0 0

37 Loss brought forward used against this year's profits

£ _____ · 0 0

38 Taxable profit for the year (box 36 minus box 37)

£ _____ · 0 0

39 Adjusted loss for the year – *from box O on the Working Sheet on page UKPN 14*

£ _____ · 0 0

40 Loss set off against 2010-11 total income – *this will be unusual. See notes on page UKPN 14*

£ _____ · 0 0

41 Loss to carry forward to following year, including unused losses brought forward

£ _____ · 0 0

Foreign

The supplementary pages headed *Foreign* cover all savings or property income, pensions and benefits that you receive from abroad.

To fill in these sections of the tax return you may need:

Business accounts and records	
Pension and social security advice notes	
Dividend and interest statements	
Property records and rents received records	
Contract notes for investment transactions	
Foreign tax payment details	

Do not declare earnings from work done abroad in this section. These must be declared in either the *Employment*, *Self-employment* or *Partnership* supplementary pages.

If you have made capital gains or losses, then these should be declared on the *Capital gains* supplementary pages, although any foreign tax incurred should be stated here.

Tax rules and regulations concerning foreign income are particularly complex – you will need to refer to the extensive notes that come with the tax return. See in particular page 77 of this book.

HM Revenue & Customs

Foreign

Tax year 6 April 2010 to 5 April 2011

The *Foreign notes* explain how to give details of your foreign income and gains on these pages. If you need more help please contact us or go to **www.hmrc.gov.uk**

- Page F 1 covers unremittable income and the claim to Foreign Tax Credit Relief.
- Pages F 2 and F 3 are for foreign savings income such as interest, dividends, pensions and social security benefits and income received by a person abroad.
- Pages F 4 and F 5 are for foreign property income.
- Page F 6 is for claiming Foreign Tax Credit Relief on income and capital gains included elsewhere on your tax return; and for entering other overseas income, gains from offshore funds and gains on foreign life insurance policies.

Unremittable income

1 If you were unable to transfer any of your overseas income to the UK, put 'X' in the box - *read page FN 3 of the notes and give details in the 'Any other information' box on your tax return or on a separate sheet*

Foreign Tax Credit Relief

If foreign tax was taken off your foreign income you may be able to claim Foreign Tax Credit Relief. Read pages FN 3 and FN 4 of the *notes* to see if you can claim the relief and how you should make the claim.

If you are calculating your tax bill you may also want to calculate your Foreign Tax Credit Relief. If you do, use the Working Sheet provided in Helpsheet 263 *Calculating Foreign Tax Credit Relief on income* and fill in box 2.

2 If you are calculating your tax, enter the total Foreign Tax Credit Relief on your income

£

Income from overseas sources

If you have income from overseas savings, foreign dividends, overseas pensions or benefits, or income, dividends received by an overseas income or country. The country or territory codes are on pages FN 19 to FN 21 of the *notes*. If there are not enough rows, attach a

A Country or territory code	B Amount of income arising or received before any tax taken off	C Foreign tax taken off or paid
Interest and other income from overseas savings		
	£	£
	£	£
	£	£
	£	£
	£	£
Dividends from foreign companies		
	£	£
	£	£
	£	£
	£	£
	£	£
	£	£
Overseas pensions, social security benefits and royalties, etc. – *read pages FN 9 and FN 10 of the notes*		
	£	£
	£	£

Dividend income received by a person abroad – *read Helpsheet 262*
if you are omitting income from this section because you are claiming an exemption, see box 46

	£	£

All other income received by a person abroad and any remitted 'ring fenced' foreign income – *read Helpsheet 262*
if you are omitting income from this section because you are claiming an exemption, see box 46

	£	£

D Special Withholding Tax and any UK tax taken off	E To claim Foreign Tax Credit Relief put 'X' in the box	F Taxable amount – *if you are claiming Foreign Tax Credit Relief, copy column B here. If not, enter column B minus column C*
£		£
£		£
£		£
£		£
£		£

Income from land and property abroad

If you have income from furnished holiday accommodation in a European Economic Area (EEA) country please enter the details

If you have overseas let properties in more than one country, or if any foreign tax has been taken off, take a copy of these pages and fill have one overseas let property, or you have more than one but they are all in the same country, you can just complete these pages.

Income and expenses

14 Total rents and other receipts (excluding taxable premiums for the grant of a lease)
£

15 Number of overseas let properties

16 Premiums paid for the grant of a lease
£

17 Property expenses (rent, repairs, legal fees, cost of services provided) – *enter the total amount*
£

18 Net profit or loss (box 14 + box 16 minus box 17) – *if this is a negative figure (a loss) put a minus sign in the box*
£

Summary

If you have filled in any of boxes 14 to 24, enter the details below.

A Country or territory code	B Adjusted profit or loss (from box 24)	C Foreign tax taken off or paid
	£	£
	£	£
	£	£
	£	£
	£	£

25 Total of column above
£

26 Total loss brought forward from earlier years
£

27 Total taxable profits (if box 25 minus box 26 is a positive amount)
£

28 Total foreign tax
£

Losses

31 Loss set off against total income – *read page FN 14 of the notes*
£

32 Total loss to carry forward to the following year – *read page FN 15 of the notes*
£

Calculating profits and losses for tax purposes

19 Private use adjustment – *read page FN 12 of the notes*
£

20 Balancing charges – *read page FN 12 of the notes*
£

21 Capital allowances for equipment and vehicles (but not for furnished residential lettings)
£

22 Landlord's energy saving allowance
£

23 10% wear and tear allowance (for furnished residential lettings only)
£

24 Adjusted profit or loss for the year (box 18 + box 19 + box 20 minus (boxes 21 to 23))
£

Foreign tax paid on employment, self-employment and other income

If you are claiming Foreign Tax Credit Relief on income included elsewhere in your tax return, fill in the columns below and say in the 'Any other information' box (on page TR 6) where on your tax return this income is included. The country or territory codes are on pages FN 19 to FN 21 of the *notes*.

A Country or territory code	C Foreign tax paid	E To claim Foreign Tax Credit Relief put 'X' in the box	F Taxable amount - *read page FN 15 of the notes*
	£		£
	£		£
	£		£
	£		£

Capital gains – Foreign Tax Credit Relief and Special Withholding Tax

If you have completed the *Capital gains summary* pages and you have paid foreign tax on those gains, and you want to claim Foreign Tax Credit Relief for the foreign tax, fill in boxes 33 to 40 below.

33 Amount of chargeable gain under UK rules
£

34 Number of days over which UK gain accrued

35 Amount of chargeable gain under foreign tax rules
£

36 Number of days over which foreign gain accrued

37 Foreign tax paid
£

38 To claim Foreign Tax Credit Relief, put 'X' in the box

39 Total Foreign Tax Credit Relief on gains
£

40 Special Withholding Tax
£

Other overseas income and gains

41 Gains on disposals of holdings in offshore funds (excluding the amounts entered in box 13) and discretionary income from non-resident trusts - *enter the amount of the gain or payment*
£

42 If you have received a benefit from a person abroad, enter the value or payment received - *if you are omitting income from this section because you are claiming an exemption, see box 46*
£

43 Gains on foreign life insurance policies, etc. (excluding the amounts entered in box 13) - *enter the amount of the gain*
£

44 Number of years

45 Tax treated as paid - *read page FN 17 of the notes*
£

46 If you have omitted income from boxes 11, 13 and 42 because you are claiming an exemption in relation to a transfer of assets, enter the total amount omitted (and give full details in the 'Any other information' box on your tax return)
£

Trusts, etc.

The supplementary pages headed Trusts etc. enable you to declare any income that you received from trusts, settlements or estates of deceased persons.

To fill in these sections you may need:

Dividend and interest statements from the trustees or personal representatives (form R185 in particular)	
Correspondence identifying the type of trust, etc.	

Tax deducted from such income may be at varying tax rates and you need to identify these in the relevant boxes of the tax return. The trustees will identify the type of tax rate that has been applied.

See also page 87 for further background information.

HM Revenue & Customs

Trusts etc.

Tax year 6 April 2010 to 5 April 2011

Your name

Your Unique Taxpayer Reference (UTR)

Income from trusts and settlements

Read the notes on pages TN 1 and TN 2 before completing these sections.

Discretionary income payment from a UK resident trust

1 Net amount – *after tax taken off*

£ · 0 0

2 Total payments from settlor-interested trusts

£ · 0 0

Non-discretionary income entitlement from a trust

3 Net amount of non-savings income – *after tax taken off*

£ · 0 0

5 Net amount of dividend income – *after tax taken off*

£ · 0 0

4 Net amount of savings income – *after tax taken off*

£ · 0 0

6 If you have included in your tax return income from trusts or settlements whose trustees are not resident in the UK for tax purposes, put 'X' in the box

---

Income chargeable on settlors

Read the notes on pages TN 2 and TN 3 before completing this section.

7 Net amount of non-savings income taxed at basic rate – *after tax taken off*

£ [   ] · [0] [0]

8 Net amount of savings income taxed at basic rate – *after tax taken off*

£ [   ] · [0] [0]

9 Net amount of dividend income taxed at dividend rate – *after tax taken off*

£ [   ] · [0] [0]

10 Net amount of non-savings income taxed at trust rate – *after tax taken off*

£ [   ] · [0] [0]

11 Net amount of savings income taxed at trust rate – *after tax taken off*

£ [   ] · [0] [0]

12 Net amount of dividend income taxed at dividend trust rate – *after tax taken off*

£ [   ] · [0] [0]

13 Non-savings income paid gross

£ [   ] · [0] [0]

14 Savings income paid gross

£ [   ] · [0] [0]

15 Additional tax paid by the trustees on certain UK life insurance policy etc. gains – *read page TN 2 of the notes*

£ [   ] · [0] [0]

Income from the estates of deceased persons

Read the notes on pages TN 3 to TN 7 before completing these sections.

Income from UK estates

16 Non-savings income – *after tax taken off*

£ [   ] · [0] [0]

17 Savings income – *after tax taken off*

£ [   ] · [0] [0]

18 Dividend income – *after tax taken off*

£ [   ] · [0] [0]

19 Non-savings income taxed at non-repayable basic rate – *after tax taken off*

£ [   ] · [0] [0]

20 Income taxed at 22% – *after tax taken off*

£ [   ] · [0] [0]

21 Dividend income taxed at non-payable dividend rate – *after tax taken off*

£ [   ] · [0] [0]

Income from foreign estates

22 Foreign estate income

£ [   ] · [0] [0]

23 Relief for UK tax already accounted for

£ [   ] · [0] [0]

Foreign tax paid on estate income

24 Foreign tax for which Foreign Tax Credit Relief has not been claimed

£ [   ] · [0] [0]

Any other information

25 Please give any other information in this space

[   ]

Capital gains summary

The supplementary pages headed *Capital gains* cover all capital gains and losses on all assets in the UK, and overseas, if you are resident and domiciled in the UK.

You have to fill in these sheets if you sold or gave away assets worth more than £40,400 and/or your net chargeable gains for tax purposes after the deduction of current year losses were £10,100 or more in the year ended 5 April 2011 or you want to claim a capital loss or make any other election.

To complete this section of the return you will need:

Copies of contract notes for the sale and purchase of shares	
Invoices and letters about the purchase and sale of other assets	
Invoices for all allowable expenses you can claim	

Chapter 15 (see page 136) covers all aspects of capital gains.

When you receive the capital gains pages there will also be capital gains summary notes and help sheets. If you have only a few transactions, this section of the tax return need not be too difficult to complete and you may well be under the parameters mentioned above in any case. If you have a great number of transactions it may well be wise to get professional help. It is almost unbelievable just how complicated capital gains tax has become over recent years, although the abolition of tapering relief and the introduction of a flat rate of capital gains tax have certainly simplified some of the calculations.

HM Revenue & Customs

Capital gains summary

Tax year 6 April 2010 to 5 April 2011

1 Your name

2 Your Unique Taxpayer Reference (UTR)

Summary of your enclosed computations

Read the notes on pages CGN 10 to CGN 12 before completing this section. You **must** enclose your computations, including details of each gain or loss, as well as filling in the boxes.

3 Total gains before 23 June 2010

£ · 0 0

4 Gains from 23 June 2010 qualifying for Entrepreneurs' Relief - *read the notes on page CGN 12*

£ · 0 0

5 Other gains from 23 June 2010

£ · 0 0

6 Total losses of the year - *enter '0' if there are none*

£ · 0 0

7 Losses brought forward and used in the year

£ · 0 0

8 Adjustment to Capital Gains Tax - *see notes*

£ · 0 0

9 Additional liability in respect of non-resident or dual resident trusts

£ · 0 0

10 Losses available to be carried forward to later years

£ · 0 0

11 Losses used against an earlier year's gain (special circumstances apply - *read the notes on page CGN 13*)

£ · 0 0

12 Losses used against income - *amount claimed against 2010-11 income*

£ · 0 0

13 Losses used against income - *amount claimed against 2009-10 income*

£ · 0 0

14 Income losses of 2010-11 set against gains

£ · 0 0

15 Gains before 23 June 2010 qualifying for Entrepreneurs' Relief - *read the notes on page CGN 14*

£ · 0 0

Listed shares and securities

16 Number of disposals - *read the notes on page CGN 14*

17 Disposal proceeds

£ · 0 0

18 Allowable costs (including purchase price)

£ · 0 0

19 Gains in the year, before losses

£ · 0 0

20 If you are making any claim or election, put 'X' in the box

21 If your computations include any estimates or valuations, put 'X' in the box

Unlisted shares and securities

22 Number of disposals - *read the notes on page CGN 15*

23 Disposal proceeds

£ [   ] . 0 0

24 Allowable costs (including purchase price)

£ [   ] . 0 0

25 Gains in the year, before losses

£ [   ] . 0 0

26 If you are making any claim or election, put 'X' in the box

27 If your computations include any estimates or valuations, put 'X' in the box

Property and other assets and gains

28 Number of disposals

29 Disposal proceeds

£ [   ] . 0 0

30 Allowable costs (including purchase price)

£ [   ] . 0 0

31 Gains in the year, before losses

£ [   ] . 0 0

32 Attributed gains before 23 June 2010 where personal losses cannot be set off

£ [   ] . 0 0

33 Attributed gains from 23 June 2010 where personal losses cannot be set off

£ [   ] . 0 0

34 If you are making any claim or election, put 'X' in the box

35 If your computations include any estimates or valuations, put 'X' in the box

Any other information

36 Please give any other information in this space

Residence, remittance basis, etc.

These supplementary pages contain a sequence of questions to enable the tax office to determine or confirm your status as regards residence and domicile.

The rules governing the legal status of a person and the consequent tax implications are among some of the most difficult in our tax legislation and are outside the scope of this basic tax guide.

However, if you have requested these supplementary pages, the tax office will automatically send you a set of extensive notes and flowcharts to help you decide your tax status. If these have not been sent to you, ask your tax office for leaflet IR211 or download it from the internet from www.hmrc.gov.uk.

Remember that you are not liable to UK tax if you go abroad to work or live for a period which will span a complete tax year providing you curtail your trips back to the UK and they do not amount to 183 days or more per year, and they are less than an average of 91 days a year for four consecutive tax years.

HM Revenue & Customs

Residence, remittance basis etc.
Tax year 6 April 2010 to 5 April 2011

Your name

Your Unique Taxpayer Reference (UTR)

Residence status
Please read pages RRN 1 to RRN 5 of the *notes* before you fill in boxes 1 to 9.

1 If you were not resident in the UK for 2010-11, put 'X' in the box

2 If you were not ordinarily resident in the UK for 2010-11, put 'X' in the box

3 If you are requesting split-year treatment for 2010-11, put 'X' in the box

4 If you were resident in the UK for 2009-10, put 'X' in the box

5 If you were ordinarily resident in the UK for 2009-10, put 'X' in the box

6 If you arrived in the UK on or after 6 April 2010, enter the date you arrived *DD MM YYYY*

7 If you left the UK on or after 6 April 2010, enter the date you left

8 If you work full-time abroad, or if you worked full-time abroad before the date in box 6 or after the date in box 7, put 'X' in the box

9 If you have come to the UK to live or to remain here for a period of two years or more, put 'X' in the box

Time spent in the UK if you were not resident or not ordinarily resident in the UK

Please complete the boxes for the whole year unless you are requesting split-year treatment. If you are (you put 'X' in box 3) complete the boxes either for the period from 6 April 2010 until your arrival, or for the period from your departure until 5 April 2011.

10 Number of days spent in the UK during 2010-11

13 Number of workdays you spent in the UK

11 Number of days in box 10 attributed to exceptional circumstances

14 Number of days you have spent in the UK since 5 April 2007 or, if you left the UK after 5 April 2007, the number of days spent in the UK since you left

12 Number of separate occasions that you have been to the UK during 2010-11

Personal allowances for non-residents and dual residents

15 If you are entitled to claim personal allowances as a non-resident because of the terms of a Double Taxation Agreement, put 'X' in the box

17 Enter the code(s) for the country or countries of which you are a national and/or resident – see page RRN 8 of the notes

16 If you are entitled to claim personal allowances as a non-resident on some other basis, or as a dual resident remittance basis user under the terms of certain Double Taxation Agreements (see notes), put 'X' in the box

ℹ Country codes can be found in the Foreign notes. These are obtainable from www.hmrc.gov.uk or the SA Orderline.

Residence in other countries

18 Enter the code(s) for the country or countries, other than the UK, in which you were resident for tax purposes for 2010-11 – see page RRN 8 of the notes

20 Relief under Double Taxation Agreements between the UK and other countries – amount claimed because of an agreement awarding residence to another country (see Helpsheet 302)

£ [   ] · 0 0

19 If you were also resident in either or both of the countries above for 2009-10, enter the appropriate code(s) – see page RRN 8 of the notes

21 Relief claimed because of other provisions of the relevant Double Taxation Agreements (see Helpsheet 304)

£ [   ] · 0 0

If you are claiming relief in box 20 or box 21, fill in the appropriate claim form in Helpsheet 302 or 304 and send this as well.

Domicile

22 If you are domiciled outside the UK and it is relevant to your Income Tax or Capital Gains Tax liability, put 'X' in the box

23 If 2010-11 is the first year you have told us that your domicile is outside the UK, put 'X' in the box

24 If you have put 'X' in box 22 and have a domicile of origin within the UK, enter the date on which your domicile changed

25 If you were born in the UK but have never been domiciled here, put 'X' in the box

26 If you have put 'X' in box 22 and you were born outside the UK, enter the date that you came to live in the UK

Remittance basis

Substantial changes were made to the remittance basis of taxation from 6 April 2008. Read pages RRN 10 to RRN 14, covering boxes 27 to 35, and pages RRN 18 to RRN 22 in the *notes* before completing this section.

27 If you are making a claim for the remittance basis for 2010-11, put 'X' in the box

28 If your unremitted income and capital gains for 2010-11 is less than £2,000, put 'X' in the box

29 If you were UK resident for 2010-11 and for seven or more of the preceding nine tax years, put 'X' in the box *(you must also complete boxes 27, 31 and 32 - see notes)*

30 If you were under 18 on 5 April 2011, put 'X' in the box

31 Amount of income you are nominating - *please provide details in box 35*

£ · 0 0

32 Amount of capital gains you are nominating - *please provide details in box 35*

£ · 0 0

33 Adjustment to payments on account for capital gains

£ · 0 0

34 If you have remitted any nominated income or gains during 2010-11, put 'X' in the box

Any other information

Boxes 13, 14, 20, 21, 24, 31 and 32 and the 'Dual residents' and 'Temporary non-residents and the remittance basis' sections of the *notes* all contain information where further information in box 35 may be required. Please refer to the *notes* on these boxes for further information on this.

35 Please give any other information in this space

Additional information

These additional pages enclosed with your tax return cover types of income, deductions and reliefs that are less common.

Other UK income
Interest from gilt-edged and other UK securities, etc.

1 Gilt etc. interest after tax taken off	3 Gross amount before tax
£ . 0 0	£ . 0 0
2 Tax taken off	
£ . 0 0	

You would have expected this interest to be declared under the interest and dividends section of the main tax return, but it appears on these pages.

Boxes 1 and 2. If you have had tax deducted from the interest, then fill in the amount actually received in box 1 and the tax deducted in box 2.

Box 3. You can elect to have interest paid without having tax deducted on Government stocks, in which case enter the total in box 3.

Use the working sheets on page 173 of this book to keep a record of the amounts. These boxes also accommodate any profit arising from buying and selling interest-bearing securities cum dividend or ex dividend (known as accrued income profits) – you may need to refer to the notes accompanying the supplementary pages as this is a complicated subject. Also refer to page 85 of this book.

Life insurance gains

4 UK life insurance policy etc. gains on which tax was treated as paid - *the amount of the gain*	8 UK life insurance policy etc. gains from voided ISAs
£ . 0 0	£ . 0 0
5 Number of years the policy has been held or since the last gain - *whichever is less*	9 Number of years the policy was held
	10 Tax taken off box 8
6 UK life insurance policy etc. gains where no tax was treated as paid - *the amount of the gain*	£ . 0 0
£ . 0 0	11 Deficiency relief - *see notes*
7 Number of years the policy has been held or since the last gain - *whichever is less*	£ . 0 0

Boxes 4 to 11. Sometimes a taxable gain arises on a life insurance policy if it is a non-qualifying policy. Your insurance company will have told you if this is the case and will have given you a 'chargeable event' certificate showing the details that you need to fill in here.

Stock dividends, non-qualifying distributions and loans written off

12	Stock dividends - the appropriate amount in cash/cash equivalent of the share capital - *without any tax*	13	Non-qualifying distributions and close company loans written off or released
£ ⬚⬚⬚⬚⬚⬚⬚ . 0 0		£ ⬚⬚⬚⬚⬚⬚⬚ . 0 0	

Box 12. This relates to stock dividends – these are offers of shares taken up instead of receiving a cash dividend. You will have received a dividend statement to this effect from the company involved and this is the amount you need to declare in this box.

Box 13. This is for non-qualifying dividends that you may have received – effectively a payment made instead of a dividend that is regarded by the tax office as being taxable. Again, you will have received a statement from the company paying the dividend to this effect. If you have received a loan from a close company and it has been written off, then this 'benefit' is taxable and should be included in box 13.

Business receipts taxed as income of an earlier year

14	The amount of post-cessation or other business receipts	15	Tax year income to be taxed, for example 2009-10 *YYYY YY*
£ ⬚⬚⬚⬚⬚⬚⬚ . 0 0		⬚⬚⬚⬚ – ⬚⬚	

Box 14. There may be circumstances where you received some late income relating to a business that had previously ceased and which, had it been received whilst the business was still trading, would have been taxable. Box 14 enables you to declare such post-cessation receipts.

Box 15. State the year to which the receipt would have originally related.

Share schemes and employment lump sums, compensation and deductions

Share schemes

1 Share schemes - the taxable amount - *excluding amounts included on your P60 or P45* £ · 0 0	**8** Exemptions for amounts entered in box 4 £ · 0 0
2 Tax taken off box 1 £ · 0 0	**9** Compensation and lump sum £30,000 exemption - *see page AiN 15 of the notes* £ · 0 0
3 Taxable lump sums - excluding redundancy and compensation for loss of your job - *see notes starting on page AiN 15 and Working Sheet 8* £ · 0 0	**10** Disability and foreign service deduction £ · 0 0
4 Lump sums or benefits received from an Employer Financed Retirement Benefits Scheme excluding pensions £ · 0 0	**11** Seafarers' Earnings Deduction - *the total amount (and give the names of the ships in the 'Additional information' box on page Ai 4)* £ · 0 0
5 Redundancy and other lump sums and compensation payments £ · 0 0	**12** Foreign earnings not taxable in the UK £ · 0 0
6 Tax taken off boxes 3 to 5 £ · 0 0	**13** Foreign tax for which tax credit relief not claimed £ · 0 0
7 If you have left box 6 blank because the tax is included in box 2 on the *Employment* page, put 'X' in the box	**14** Exempt employers' contributions to an overseas pension scheme £ · 0 0

Boxes 1 and 2. In previous years there were supplementary pages specifically for share schemes but now you have to declare any taxable amount in these 'additional information' pages here.

The general background information on share schemes is given on pages 76–77 of this book. However, the rules and regulations vary from scheme to scheme and they can be very complex, as will be seen from the working notes accompanying your tax return. You must use a separate set of sheets for each share scheme.

It is important that you consult your employer or the trustees of your scheme if you require help or clarification before filling in this section of the tax return.

These boxes only cover any liability to income tax; if you have made capital gains or losses on disposing of your holdings you may need to declare them in the Capital gains supplementary pages.

Taxable lump sums, compensation for loss of office and redundancy
Boxes 3 to 10. In negotiating termination or compensation of any kind with your employer, the question of what is and what is not going to be liable to tax should be discussed in full, preferably with independent

advisers. Enter the details here. On page 74, there is general and tax advice covering these matters.

Seafarers' earnings deduction

Box 11. A deduction from earnings (a foreign earnings deduction) is available to seafarers working on a ship who have an eligible period of absence from the UK.

Fill in the amount (which your employer should provide) in box 11 and the names of the ships in box 20 (see page 66).

Foreign earnings not taxable in the UK

Most matters relating to overseas earnings are covered in the *Residence* supplementary pages (see page 57) and the *Foreign* supplementary pages (see page 48) but surprisingly there are elements of earnings that need to be recorded here.

The whole issue of residence and domicile is very complicated and outside the scope of this book. You are advised to seek professional help to ensure you do not pay more tax than you should. There are copious notes issued by HMRC (help sheet 211) which you can obtain by telephoning 0845 9000 404.

Exempt employers' contributions to an overseas pension scheme

Box 14. This enables you to state the amount if you think your employer has made any such contributions. Your employer should provide you with a statement to this effect at the end of the tax year.

Other tax reliefs

1 Subscriptions for Venture Capital Trust shares - *the amount on which relief is claimed*	**6** Post-cessation expenses and certain other losses
£ . 0 0	£ . 0 0
2 Subscriptions for shares under the Enterprise Investment Scheme - *the amount on which relief is claimed (and provide more information on page Ai 4)*	**7** Maintenance payments (max £2,670) - *only if you or your former spouse or civil partner were born before 6 April 1935*
£ . 0 0	£ . 0 0
3 Community Investment Tax Relief - *the amount on which relief is claimed*	**8** Payments to a trade union etc. for death benefits - *half the amount paid (max £100)*
£ . 0 0	£ . 0 0
4 UK royalties and annual payments made	**9** Relief claimed for employer's compulsory widow's, widower's or orphan's benefit scheme - *(max £20)*
£ . 0 0	£ . 0 0
5 Qualifying loan interest payable in the year	**10** Relief claimed on a qualifying distribution on the redemption of bonus shares or securities
£ . 0 0	£ . 0 0

Boxes 1, 2 and 3. Information about venture capital trusts and enterprise investment schemes can be found on pages 162 and 163 of this book, as well as community investment tax relief.

Box 4. See page 92.

Box 5. Qualifying interest is dealt with on page 89.

Box 6. Any *income* you have received after your business ceased trading is dealt with on page 128; conversely you may have had to make later *payments* which are allowed for tax and it is in box 6 that you can claim these.

Box 7. See page 90.

Boxes 8 and 9. See page 92.

Box 10. If you are a higher-rate tax payer and have redeemed bonus shares then such payment will have included a tax credit but the receipt of such distribution will have already been declared by you in the dividends box (box 3) on page TR3 of the main tax return. If you do not fill in box 10, then you will be taxed twice on the distribution.

Age-related married couple's allowance

If you, or your spouse or civil partner, were born **before** 6 April 1935, complete the relevant boxes

1 Your spouse's or civil partner's full name

2 Their date of birth if older than you (and at least one of you was born before 6 April 1935) *DD MM YYYY*

3 If you have already agreed that **half** the minimum allowance is to go to your spouse or civil partner, put 'X' in the box

4 If you have already agreed that **all** of the minimum allowance is to go to your spouse or civil partner, put 'X' in the box

5 If, in the year to 5 April 2011, you lived with any previous spouse or civil partner, enter their date of birth

6 If you have already agreed that **half** of the minimum allowance is to be given to you, put 'X' in the box

7 If you have already agreed that **all** of the minimum allowance is to be given to you, put 'X' in the box

8 Your spouse's or civil partner's full name

9 If you were married or formed a civil partnership after 5 April 2010, enter the date of marriage or civil partnership *DD MM YYYY*

10 If you want to have your spouse's or civil partner's surplus allowance, put 'X' in the box

11 If you want your spouse or civil partner to have your surplus allowance, put 'X' in the box

Boxes 1 to 11. Here you can claim the married couple's allowance if either you, your husband or wife or civil partner were born before 6 April 1935; see page 95 for further details and the opportunities for transferring all or part of this allowance to your partner if it will save you tax. Provided one of the partners was born before 6 April 1935 and you married or formed a civil partnership during the tax year, you can claim a proportion of the annual allowance pro-rata.

Other information
Income tax losses

Other income losses	Trading losses
1 Earlier years' losses – *which can be set against certain other income in 2010-11* £ ▢▢▢▢▢▢▢ . 0 0	**3** Relief now for 2011-12 trading, or certain capital, losses £ ▢▢▢▢▢▢▢ . 0 0
2 Total unused losses carried forward £ ▢▢▢▢▢▢▢ . 0 0	**4** Tax year for which you are claiming relief in box 3, for example 2009-10 *YYYY YY* ▢▢▢▢ – ▢▢

See page 128 regarding losses and the figures to go in this section of the tax return.

Pension savings tax charges and taxable lump sums from overseas pension schemes

5 Value of pension benefits in excess of your Available Lifetime Allowance, taken by you as a lump sum £ ▢▢▢▢▢▢▢ . 0 0	**12** Amount of unauthorised payment from a pension scheme, subject to Surcharge £ ▢▢▢▢▢▢▢ . 0 0
6 Value of pension benefits in excess of your Available Lifetime Allowance, not taken as a lump sum £ ▢▢▢▢▢▢▢ . 0 0	**13** Foreign tax paid on an unauthorised payment (in £ sterling) £ ▢▢▢▢▢▢▢ . 0 0
7 Lifetime Allowance tax paid by your pension scheme £ ▢▢▢▢▢▢▢ . 0 0	**14** Taxable short service refund of contributions (overseas pension schemes only) £ ▢▢▢▢▢▢▢ . 0 0
8 Amount saved towards your pension, in the period covered by this tax return, in excess of the Annual Allowance £ ▢▢▢▢▢▢▢ . 0 0	**15** Taxable lump sum death benefit payment (overseas pension schemes only) £ ▢▢▢▢▢▢▢ . 0 0
9 Amount saved towards your pension in excess of the Special Annual Allowance taxed at 20% £ ▢▢▢▢▢▢▢ . 0 0	**16** Taxable refunds of contributions (overseas pension schemes only) £ ▢▢▢▢▢▢▢ . 0 0
10 Amount saved towards your pension in excess of the Special Annual Allowance taxed at 30% £ ▢▢▢▢▢▢▢ . 0 0	**17** Foreign tax paid (in £ sterling) on boxes 14, 15 and 16 £ ▢▢▢▢▢▢▢ . 0 0
11 Amount of unauthorised payment from a pension scheme, not subject to surcharge £ ▢▢▢▢▢▢▢ . 0 0	

Pages 163–167 of this book deal with pension contributions and elements of the pension legislation that can give rise to tax charges. It is unlikely that this section of the tax return will apply unless you have a very high-value pension fund or one to which you are making very large annual contributions.

Tax avoidance schemes

18 The scheme reference number	19 The tax year in which the expected advantage arises, for example 2009-10 *YYYY YY*
☐☐☐☐☐☐☐☐	☐☐☐☐ – ☐☐
☐☐☐☐☐☐☐☐	☐☐☐☐ – ☐☐

Boxes 18 and 19. These enable you to declare details of any tax avoidance schemes in which you have been involved. You should consult a qualified adviser as to the information required.

Additional information

20 Please give any additional information in this space

Personal details

21 Your name	22 Your Unique Taxpayer Reference (UTR)
	☐☐☐☐☐ ☐☐☐☐☐

Box 20. You can use this box to give more details about items already declared in these sheets if it will add clarity to the tax office understanding the figures, and thus prevent unnecessary correspondence.

CHAPTER 5

Your 2011 tax return

Employment income, benefits and pensions

This chapter deals with income from employment including any benefits or expense allowances, and redundancy or leaving compensation you have received. Any pensions and social security benefits received are also covered here.

Your earnings and benefits from employment and pension income have to be declared in the *Employment* supplementary pages.

Wages, salaries, fees, bonuses, etc.

You should have received from your employer a form P60 which shows your earnings for the year and tax deducted under PAYE. You are entitled by law to receive this form by 31 May so do chase your employer if it is not to hand.

Also include in the *Employment* pages of the tax return any salary you received from your husband or wife or civil partner if you were employed in his or her business. You must show your gross earnings before any deductions of income tax and national insurance, but you are allowed to deduct any contributions you make to your employer's pension scheme provided that it is one approved by the tax inspector, or any payroll giving donations.

If your P60 form includes an amount for jobseeker's allowance then, confusingly, this should be shown in box 14 in the Income section of your main tax return. The P60 form may also show earnings from a previous employer, in which case show your current earnings in the boxes on the first page of the Employment pages and previous earnings in the boxes on the second page.

Directors' remuneration is frequently voted on an annual basis. The amount to declare in your tax return is usually the amount actually received in the tax year (normally the figure on your P60 form); however, you are taxable on earnings shown in the company's accounts if such sums were available (even if not actually drawn by you) in the tax year.

In addition to your regular PAYE employment, you may have other earnings. These might include casual work, fees and commissions, etc. Providing these incomes are not paid at regular intervals nor paid by the same person, then it is unlikely they will be classed as employment income. Do not enter such income in the *Employment* pages but under the Income section of the main tax return (box 16) – see page 27 of this book. Make sure you claim any relevant expenses in box 17.

Tips and gratuities, if not included in your P60 form, should be shown in box 3 of the *Employment* pages.

Benefits

Company cars

Virtually all employees whose earnings and reimbursed expenses, including potential benefits in kind, are at the rate of £8,500 a year or more, and all directors whatever their earnings and expenses, are liable to pay tax on any benefit they have from the use of a company car, and additionally on any fuel used on private journeys if paid for by their employer. These benefits will still be taxable if the car is used by a member of the employee's family or household. Company car and fuel benefits should appear in your coding notice or tax assessment and need to be checked against the information provided by your employer on your annual P11D form.

The car benefit tax applies to all company cars, including those that are leased, and will be assumed by your tax office to cover all the running costs, even if these amount to more than the tax benefit charge. The cost of a chauffeur, however, will be taxed as a separate benefit.

If your employer pays your congestion charges in London (or elsewhere) they are not regarded as a separate taxable benefit as they are considered to be covered in the taxable benefit you pay on the vehicle.

A taxable benefit will not usually arise if a company car is part of a 'pool', provided that the vehicle is actually used by two or more employees, with any private use being merely incidental, and the vehicle is not normally kept overnight at or near the employee's place of residence.

If a company car is not available for a period of at least 30 consecutive days (for example, if it is in for repair), then the car benefit is reduced proportionately.

Company car benefit

The tax charge on a company car benefit is calculated as a percentage of the list price of the car, but this percentage is graduated according to carbon dioxide (CO_2) emissions.

The table on page 70 shows the benefit charges. The minimum charge will be 5 per cent of the list price for cars with the lowest CO_2 emissions with a maximum of 35 per cent for cars with high emissions. Ask the tax office for leaflet IR172 if you require more information.

Your car's emission figure will either be in the vehicle registration document or available from the manufacturer or dealer, or via the vehicle enquiry link **www.taxdisc.gov.uk**.

There is no reduction for business mileage or the age of the car.

The value of the vehicle for tax purposes is the manufacturer's list price at the time of first registration (less any personal contribution up to £5,000) and including delivery charges, VAT and any accessories over £100 added to the vehicle, unless they were for disabled persons. There was a cap of £80,000 on the list, or market, price but this was abolished in the 2011 budget.

There are exceptions for classic cars; the open market value is taken instead of the list price where the car is aged 15 years or more at the end of the tax year and has a market value of £15,000 or more.

Company car private fuel benefit

If your employer pays for fuel used on your private journeys (and this includes travel from home to your normal business address), then you are taxed on this benefit regardless of your annual business mileage.

A standard figure of £18,000 is used (increasing to £18,800 from April 2011) and the tax benefit is based on the CO_2 rating percentage of your vehicle (see table on page 70). For example, if you had a vehicle that used petrol with CO_2 emissions of 180 for 2010–2011, then the taxable benefit will be 25 per cent × £18,000 = £4,500.

The tax charge is the maximum that can be levied, even if in practice the cost of private mileage is more.

Is there any way you can avoid the fuel tax charge? Yes – you can pay for all your own private fuel (or reimburse your employer for all the private usage) but if you do this you will have to keep a detailed record each year of every car journey undertaken, both private and business. Bear in mind that travel from your home to your normal place of business is considered to be private mileage for tax purposes. You may well find it to your advantage to accept the tax charge – it might be less than you would actually pay for private mileage!

Cars with approved CO_2 emissions rating
CO_2 emissions in grammes per kilometre
(rounded down to the nearest multiple)

CO_2	2010–2011		2011–2012	
	Petrol %	*Diesel* %	*Petrol* %	*Diesel* %
75 or less	5	8	5	8
76-120	10	13	10	13
121-129	15	18	15	18
130-134	15	18	16	19
135-139	16	19	17	20
140-144	17	20	18	21
145-149	18	21	19	22
150-154	19	22	20	23
155-159	20	23	21	24
160-164	21	24	22	25
165-169	22	25	23	26
170-174	23	26	24	27
175-179	24	27	25	28
180-184	25	28	26	29
185-189	26	29	27	30
190-194	27	30	28	31
195-199	28	31	29	32
200-204	29	32	30	33
205-209	30	33	31	34
210-214	31	34	32	35
215-219	32	35	33	35
220-224	33	35	34	35
225-229	34	35	35	35
230 plus	35	35	35	35

Notes

There will be further tightening of this benefit from April 2012.

1 Cars and vans with zero emissions (e.g. electric vehicles) do not have a taxable benefit.

2 The 2010–2011 figures in this chart are reduced by 3 per cent for cars run on hybrid electricity/petrol and 2 per cent for those run on bio-ethanol. These discounts ceased from 6 April 2011.

3 Ultra low carbon vehicles (under 75 CO_2) have a 5 per cent benefit charge.

Mileage allowances

If you use your own car on your employer's business you can claim authorised mileage rates of 40p per mile (45p from 1 June 2011) for the first 10,000 business miles in a tax year, and 25p a mile thereafter; any payment over these figures will be subject to tax and national insurance.

If your employer reimburses less than the mileage figure above, you can claim the difference in your tax return. An extra 5p per mile can be paid by your employer if you have a business passenger, but you cannot claim relief for this if your employer doesn't pay this.

You will only need to declare in your tax return the mileage payments you receive if they are in excess of these approved figures. The motorcycle rates are 24p per business mile and 20p for bicycles and have remained at these figures since 2007–2008.

If you use a company car and *you* provide the fuel for business travel, you can claim reimbursement from your employer at the following maximum rates per mile from 1 June 2011 (previous figures in brackets) without incurring any taxable benefit.

Company car mileage allowances on own fuel		
	Petrol	*LPG*
1400cc or less	15p (11p)	11p (7p)
1400–2000cc	18p (14p)	13p (8p)
Over 2000cc	26p (20p)	18p (18p)
	Diesel	
1600cc or less	12p (11p 1400cc or less)	
1600–2000cc	15p (11p 1400–2000cc)	
Over 2000cc	18p (14p over 2000cc)	

Company vans

Employees benefiting from the private use of a company van pay income tax on a standard 'benefit' of £3,000 a year irrespective of the age of the van. The benefit is apportioned in the case of shared vans.

If you use the van for unrestricted private use, you also pay tax on a fuel benefit of £500 (£550 for 2011–12) a year but there is no charge where fuel is provided only for home to work journeys.

Bicycles

Under this scheme your employer can provide you with a cut price bicycle if you cycle to work.

Most cycle retailers take part in this scheme; your employer pays for the bike (and accessories) – (there is no limit so you can get an expensive one if your employer agrees!) – and leases it back to you over say a 12-month period for an agreed nominal amount. The amount you pay is deducted from your gross salary before tax and national insurance (so this reduces these tax charges); at the end of the lease period, the employer 'sells' the bike to you for a pre-agreed nominal amount on which you will not pay tax. You can't claim the 20p a mile (see above) whilst you lease but you can once you own the bike.

Bear in mind this salary sacrifice, as it is called, could affect either your earnings figure if you are borrowing for a mortgage or your pension entitlement, but the figures should not be significant.

Living accommodation

Unless there are exceptional circumstances, living accommodation provided by an employer is taxable as a benefit.

The amount assessed will normally equate to the gross rateable value of the property, but if the cost of the property is higher than £75,000 then an additional amount is taxable, based on the market value of the property, less £75,000, multiplied by the official rate of interest which is announced, and varied, by HMRC periodically. Any rent or contribution to upkeep you made to your employer is deductible from the benefit before calculating tax due. You will, however, be assessed on any expenditure paid on your behalf (for example, heating, council tax, etc.).

Low-interest loan

An employee earning above £8,500 a year (see below) who has the benefit of a cheap or interest-free loan is taxable on the benefit as compared with the official rate of interest (available from your tax office). Your employer does not need to report loans if the whole of the interest would have been liable for tax relief. If the total of non-eligible loans does not exceed £5,000 at any time in the tax year or if the loan is made on commercial terms and your employer supplies goods or services on credit to the general public, then no charge is made.

Other benefits

All employees whose earnings, expenses and potential benefits are at the rate of £8,500 a year or more, and most directors regardless of their earnings or expenses, will probably have had any benefits or perks they have received reported to the tax inspector by their employer. The employer has to do this by law by sending in a form P11D, a copy of which you are entitled to receive by 6 July. However, it is still your responsibility to declare such a perk in your tax return. There are certain benefits or perks that an employer can provide which are tax free. You need not mention them on your tax return if they are not taxable, but see page 82 for dispensations, etc.

Some of the more usual benefits, with a summary of the tax situation, are detailed below.

Benefit	Benefits	
	Employees earning £8,500 a year or more and directors	*Employees earning less than £8,500 a year*
Armed forces operational allowance	Not taxable	
Assets provided for your use free of charge (e.g. video)	Taxable at 20 per cent of initial market value	Usually tax free
Bicycles	See page 71	
Canteen facilities	Not taxable if available to all staff	
Car and bike parking at work	Not taxable	
Cash vouchers	Taxable	
Child care costs and vouchers	Not taxable up to £55 per week (but see page 153)	
Clothing and other goods given by your employer	Taxable	Taxed on secondhand value
Company cars, vans, etc.	Taxable	Not taxable
Computer equipment	Not taxable on first £2,500 of value	
Credit cards (for personal, not business expenditure)	Taxable	
Exam prizes	Not taxable if reasonable and not part of employment contract	
Fuel for private use of car	Taxable	Not taxable
Holidays	Taxable	If employer pays directly, tax-free
Interest-free loan	Normally taxable	Not taxable
In-house benefits	Taxable on value of the marginal or additional cost to the employer	
Living accommodation	Normally taxable unless essential for your employment	

Benefit	Employees earning £8,500 a year or more and directors	Employees earning less than £8,500 a year
Loan of computers	Not taxable if less than £2,500	
Luncheon vouchers	Tax free up to 15p per working day	
Mileage allowances	Tax free up to the authorised rates – any excess is taxable	
Mobile telephones	Not taxable if employer provides	
Nurseries and play schemes run by employer	Not taxable if at employer's premises or, if elsewhere, financed by employer	
Outplacement counselling	Not taxable	
Pension contributions and death-in-service cover	Normally tax-free	
Private health schemes	Taxable	Not taxable if company scheme
Prizes/incentive awards	Taxable	Not taxable
Relocation expenses	Tax-free up to £8,000 (if qualifying)	
Retraining and counselling on leaving employment	Not taxable if you have been employed for at least two years	
Scholarships provided by employers' trust	Taxable	
Season tickets for travel paid directly by employer	Taxable	
Share incentive schemes	Not taxable if approved by HMRC	
Sick pay schemes	Taxable	
Travel to work by bus (free or discounted)	Not taxable in qualifying circumstances	
Workplace sports facilities	Not taxable	

Leaving payments and compensation

Compensation for loss of office, payment in lieu of notice, ex-gratia payments, redundancy pay and retirement and death lump sums all come under this heading in the tax return. The relevant sections of the tax return are shown on page 62.

The first £30,000 of compensation is tax free, but any excess is taxable. This £30,000 limit has not been increased since 1988! Note, however, that if your contract of employment gives you a right to

An example of the tax calculations arising on the receipt of redundancy pay

John was made redundant during the 2010–2011 tax year. His total earnings for the year were £44,000 and he was awarded a redundancy payment of £90,000.

		£
Earnings		44,000
Less: Personal allowance, say		6,475
		37,525
Tax liability	£37,400 at 20 per cent	7,480
	125 at 40 per cent	50
	£37,525 Tax due	£7,530

A redundancy payment of £90,000 is to be made after the form P45 has been issued. The employer will deduct tax as follows:

	£
Redundancy	90,000
Less: Tax-free limit	30,000
	60,000
Less: Tax on £60,000 at 20 per cent	12,000
	£48,000

Once the employer has notified the tax office of this redundancy payment, they will then review the tax position as follows:

	£
Earnings	44,000
Add: Redundancy after tax-free limit	60,000
	104,000
Less: Personal allowance	6,475
	£97,525

Tax liability calculated as:		£
£37,400 at 20 per cent		7,480
£60,125 at 40 per cent		24,050
£97,525		31,530

	£	
Less: Tax already collected (as above)	7,530	
Deducted from redundancy payment	12,000	19,530
Additional tax due		£12,000

compensation on ceasing to be employed, then the lump sum you receive will be taxable, regardless of the amount.

When considering agreements for compensation, it is wise to consult a tax adviser or solicitor to negotiate the terms and the timing, which can be critical, especially on termination of a contract. Any benefits arising after termination will be taxed only when they are actually received or 'enjoyed', rather than being taken into account in the actual redundancy year. An example is given on page 75 of the various tax calculations that have to be considered when assessing the impact of redundancy pay.

In the example shown, when John sends in his 2011 self assessment tax return he will include the redundancy payment and will pay any tax due to the tax office by 31 January 2012.

When submitting your tax return, make sure you fill in the relevant boxes on page Ai2 of the *Additional information* supplementary pages (see page 62 in this book).

Expense allowances

Round-sum allowances are taxable as income unless an employee (and such term includes a director) can identify accurately the expenditure involved and satisfy the tax office that such sums were spent wholly, exclusively and necessarily on the employer's business.

Refer also to Chapter 6 (see page 80).

Share schemes

There are many approved share schemes that now offer tax incentives to encourage employees' involvement in companies, but the rules are complicated and vary from scheme to scheme. The relevant sections of the tax return are reproduced on page 62. Some schemes are unapproved and do not qualify for the same level of tax benefits.

The following gives a very brief summary of the main types of scheme and the tax benefits associated with them.

Savings-related share schemes (save as you earn)

Employees pay a monthly sum via their employer into a savings-related share option scheme over a predetermined period at the end of which, the savings, plus a tax-free bonus, are used to purchase shares at a fixed price. (There is a minimum of £5 a month and a maximum of £250 a month.) This price must not be less than 80 per cent of the market value at the time of the option. No income tax or national insurance is payable on the option grant or on exercising the option.

No capital gain arises if shares are transferred into an ISA within certain time limits and within the ISA maximum amount limits.

Approved share incentive plans

Employees are able to allocate part of their salary to acquire partnership shares in the company that employs them, without paying tax or national insurance, from which the employer is also exempt. Additionally, an employer can award free shares for participating employees and/or you can allocate your dividends to buy more shares. There are maximum limits depending on the type of shares and various periods of ownership required (usually five years) to benefit fully from the tax advantages.

Company share option schemes

An employer grants to an employee an option to purchase shares at a fixed price (which must not be discounted) at a future date. No income tax or national insurance is payable on the granting of the option nor on any proceeds of sale, provided you take up the option between three and ten years.

Approved profit-sharing schemes

New schemes have not been possible since 31 December 2002 but you may still be holding such free shares, which will be held by a trust on your behalf.

Enterprise management incentives

Employers can offer these incentive share options to their staff. They are normally free of income tax and both employer's and employee's national insurance, but capital gains tax may be charged.

There are tax rules and regulations that identify the type of company that can grant these incentives and a definition of employees that are eligible to receive them.

Foreign income

There are *Foreign* supplementary pages to the tax return which specifically deal with people who normally live in the UK but have savings, property income or benefits from overseas (see page 48).

There are measures intended to protect employees from paying tax twice on the same income, principally the double taxation agreements held with various countries throughout the world, and these are detailed in the notes that come with these supplementary pages. Special concessions exist for seafarers (see page 63).

If you receive a pension as a result of employment with an overseas Government, only 90 per cent of the pension is taxable (see box 10 in your main tax return).

Before you take up an appointment abroad, check carefully, both with your employer and with your tax office, as to how foreign earnings in your particular instance will be treated for tax purposes.

You will be classed as a non-resident for tax purposes if you live and work abroad for at least the whole of a tax year provided your visits back to the UK do not amount to more than 183 days in a tax year (or 91 days averaged over four years). This means that your earnings from overseas will be tax free. If you are a UK resident, any foreign earnings will be taxable in the UK.

Keep an eye on the national insurance situation – you don't want to lose your rights to UK State benefits because you have not paid enough NI contributions. Ask for HMRC leaflet N138 and DWP leaflet SA 29 which clarifies this complicated area.

Income from pensions

All your pension income, including the State retirement pension, has to be declared on page TR3 of your main tax return. Refer to page 26 of this book for advice on how to fill in the various boxes. If you have pension income from private pension schemes in addition to the State pension then it is important that you check at the end of the tax year how much tax has been deducted to see if you are due a refund. See Chapter 12, on page 115, on how to go about this.

Due to the major restructuring in the pension legislation that took place in April 2006, there may be tax liabilities if you have exceeded certain limits in terms of the value of your pension fund, or amounts of your annual pension contributions, or indeed if your pension scheme was unapproved by HMRC. Any potential liability can be declared in the *Additional information* pages of the tax return. Refer to page 165 in this book for advice.

State benefits received

It is under the *Income* section, on page TR3 of your main tax return, that you need to declare any State benefits received. The tax treatment of these benefits is extremely complicated and it would take a separate book to cover all the legislation.

However, as an overview, you need to declare in box 12 of your main tax return any taxable incapacity benefit (excepting the first 28 weeks) and in box 14 any jobseeker's allowance; declare the total of all the following benefits in box 15:
• Bereavement allowance and widow's pension.
• Widowed mother's or widowed parent's allowance.
• Carer's allowance.

EMPLOYMENT INCOME, BENEFITS AND PENSIONS

- Industrial death benefit paid as a pension.
- Statutory sick, maternity, paternity and adoption pay if paid by HMRC (if paid by your employer it would have been included in your P60 earnings declared in your *Employment* pages).

Exclude any amounts included in any of the above that are paid for child dependency or child allowance. Chapter 2 lists those social security benefits that are exempt from tax and do not have to be declared in your tax return (see page 13).

Use the working sheets at the back of this book to keep a record of the details making up the totals you declare in your tax return in case the tax office require the information at a later date.

• 79 •

CHAPTER 6

Your 2011 tax return

Claiming expenses against your income

There are certain types of expenditure which, if necessary for your job and provided at your expense, may be claimed against your income. Fill in the appropriate boxes in the expenses section of the *Employment* supplementary pages of your tax return. To assist your claim it may be worthwhile obtaining a letter from your employer confirming that whilst your expenses are justified and necessary for your job, they are not automatically reimbursed as part of your remuneration agreement.

It is important to keep a record of the details and dates on which the expenditure was incurred, and the receipts where possible. Some allowable expenses are listed below.

Factory, manual, shop and healthcare workers

Extra costs incurred by employees working temporarily away from home. Lorry drivers and construction site workers have special concessions.

- Overalls, boiler suits, boots, helmets, gloves and other special protective clothing. You should also include the cost of cleaning and repairing such items.

- Tools, toolbags and equipment.

- Travelling expenses (but see page 82).

- Trade journals and technical books essential to your job.

- Trade unions often agree with the tax inspector a fixed allowance which you can claim to cover certain expenses. Alternatively, keep a record of all your expenses and submit an annual claim.

- Working rule agreements which exist between the tax office and various construction industry representatives and healthcare workers have set guidelines regarding the expenses you can claim.

Sales representatives, office and clerical workers

- Travelling and hotel expenses on company business. If you use your own car for business travel, then you can claim the mileage allowances shown on page 71.

- Technical and other books on your firm's products or services. It may be advisable to obtain a letter from your employer confirming that this expenditure is necessary for your job.

- Telephone – part of your own telephone bill covering calls to customers, etc.

- Gifts to customers paid for by yourself which do not cost more than £50 per customer per year and which advertise your firm's products or services. (The gift must not be food, drink, tobacco or a voucher.)

- Fees or subscriptions paid to an organisation of which you are a member. The organisation must be on the HMRC approved list.

- Journals and publications essential to your employment or profession.

Seafarer's deduction

A deduction from earnings (a foreign earnings deduction) is available to seafarers working on a ship who have an eligible period of absence from the UK (see page 63).

Use of your home as an office

If you are required to do work for your employer at home, and use a specific room for this purpose, you ought to claim an allowance based on a proportion of total upkeep, for example, rent, light, heat, insurance, cleaning, repairs to furniture, etc. Such a claim should be made in box 20 'other expenses' on the *Employment* supplementary pages in your tax return. (See also pages 121 and 141 regarding business use and capital gains tax.) Your employer is able to pay a tax free and national insurance free allowance of up to £3 per week to cover the additional costs of working at home without being supported by receipts. Higher amounts must have substantive paperwork.

Capital allowances

If you use equipment such as a computer, provided by yourself, which is essential for your work, then you can claim capital allowances. This does not apply if you use your own car whilst on your employer's business – the official mileage allowance (see page 71) is considered to include a sum in lieu of capital allowances.

Travelling expenses

You are able to claim travelling expenses as a tax deduction against your income if they have not been reimbursed by your employer, provided the journeys were not repetitive, that is from your home to a permanent place of work. This means that if your work takes you to many different locations, even if you start from home each day, then such expenses can be claimed. However, if you routinely visit a different office or branch each day of the week you may establish that you have more than one permanent workplace.

The tax legislation is complicated, but where a site-based employee is working for more than 24 months at that workplace, it will be regarded as permanent and travelling expenses from home to site will not be allowed for tax.

Incidental overnight expenses

Miscellaneous personal expenses up to £5 a night paid by the employer whilst away from home on business in the UK (£10 a night abroad) are tax free.

Interest payments

If you have to borrow money to buy equipment (such as a computer) necessary for your job, then the interest can be claimed as an expense against your income. Relief for car loans is not available to individuals, nor is interest on a bank overdraft or credit card allowable.

Employees earning £8,500 or more, and directors

As explained on page 72, your employer has to send to the tax office a form P11D, which details expenses and benefits that you have received. There is a legal obligation for all employers to give their employees copies of these forms by 6 July, which will be a help in checking your tax.

Refer to Chapter 5, which covers all such benefits.

You might receive a letter from your tax office asking for details of these expenses, and you must then convince them that you did not receive any personal benefit or, if you did, obtain their agreement on the proportion of the expenses to be disallowed and on which you will pay tax.

Sometimes an employer can arrange with the tax office to get a dispensation making it unnecessary to complete certain parts of form

P11D, in which case the employee does not need to include such expenses in their tax return.

The major conditions for a dispensation are normally that the reimbursement of expenses is closely supervised and it is obvious that the expenses themselves are easily justifiable (for example, travelling and subsistence expenses for a representative).

Even if a dispensation is granted, the expenses still have to be taken into account in deciding if an employee's total remuneration, including reimbursed expenses, is £8,500 or more.

HMRC have recently stated that they are to review all dispensations that originated prior to 2004 and employers will have to complete a form P11DX; if this is not done, then HMRC will assume that the dispensation is no longer required.

An employer may also make an arrangement to meet the tax liability on behalf of employees in respect of certain benefits. This is known as a PAYE settlement agreement and may cover items such as Christmas gifts, awards and shared benefits.

CHAPTER 7

Your 2011 tax return

Income from savings, investments, property and trusts, etc.

This chapter deals with income from land and property, dividends and interest from investments and trusts and also maintenance, which you may need to declare in your tax return. This section of the tax return is shown on pages 24–25 of this book.

Assets held in joint names

If a husband and wife or civil partner have income from an asset held in joint names, it is assumed to be divided equally when filling in your respective tax returns, even if you own it in unequal shares. If the ownership is not held equally and you are entitled to the income in proportion to your share, then you should ask the tax office for form 17 on which you can jointly declare the actual ownership split. You then enter the amounts accordingly in your tax returns. Such declaration takes effect from the date it is made, provided the form is sent to the tax office within 60 days.

Interest from savings and investments

This interest has to be declared in your tax return in boxes 1 to 6. This section of the return is reproduced on page 24 of this book. You will need to differentiate between interest that has had tax deducted and that which has been paid gross. Use the working sheets at the back of this book as you only have to show the totals, not the detail, in your tax return.

If you have joint savings or investments, only include your share of the income in your tax return. Refer to page 147 as to whether you can save tax by changing some of your investments to joint holdings.

Show all your income from National Savings and investments in this section but exclude the first £70 of interest earned on any ordinary account that you may still have.

You do not have to include interest from National Savings certificates as that is tax free.

Investment account interest with National Savings is credited automatically to your account on 31 December – you can request a statement and the tax office will accept this figure to go in your return. You do not have to apportion it on a time basis.

Remember to include National Savings interest from income or capital bonds under this section of the return. The interest is taxed on an annual basis even though it is not actually received until the bond is repaid after five years. Include also details of first option bonds and fixed rate savings bonds.

There is no need to enter interest from an SAYE account as it is not taxable, nor is interest from PEPs, ISAs etc.

For a general review of savings and the tax implications see Chapter 18.

If your total income is below your personal allowances then your bank or building society does not have to deduct tax from the interest before you receive it. See page 116 as to the action you should take.

Dividends from shares in UK companies

Enter in your tax return the amounts that you actually received as shown on your dividend slips. The date on the dividend slip is considered as being the date receivable for tax return purposes. Show income from most unit trusts here, including the income that was reinvested in further units instead of being paid direct to you. The treatment of these tax credits is shown on page 105.

Scrip dividends should also be included here – the dividend statement should show 'the appropriate amount in cash', which is the dividend.

Do not include any equalisation receipts.

Purchased life annuities

These are covered in the Pensioners chapter on page 117.

Accrued income securities

Where fixed-interest securities are sold or purchased and the contract note includes an adjustment for accrued interest, this will need to be reported on your tax return unless the nominal value of all your accrued income securities does not exceed £5,000 in the tax year concerned.

The rules are complicated, but the notes accompanying your tax return will include further guidance and HMRC are looking at proposals to simplify the scheme in the future.

Property income

The tax return *UK property* supplementary pages cover all aspects of UK property income (see page 45).

If a husband and wife or civil partner own a property that is let, the tax office will assume that any income from these assets is divided equally. You should enter in your tax return one half of the income and expenses, and tick the relevant box to indicate to the tax office that it is a joint holding. If the ownership is not held equally, then refer to page 84 as to the action you should take.

For the purposes of income tax, all income from property in the UK (and in the EEA from April 2011), including furnished, unfurnished and holiday lettings, is taxable on the same commercial basis as any other business (see Chapter 13) .

However, furnished holiday lettings enjoy special tax advantages provided that certain conditions are met; these are that your property was available for letting at a commercial rent for at least 140 days in each tax year (210 days from April 2012), actually let for a minimum of 70 days (105 days from April 2012) and not rented out for a continuous period of more than 31 days to the same person in any 155-day period.

Losses prior to 6 April 2011 can be offset against total income and are not restricted to the rental business; additional capital allowances can be claimed, there is more flexible capital gains relief and relevant earnings treatment for pension purposes. From April 2011, losses can only be carried forward and offset only against future profits from holiday lettings.

Property expenses

If you receive rents from a property which you let furnished or unfurnished you can claim the following expenses, if applicable:

- Rent paid and water rates.

- General maintenance and repairs of the property, garden and furniture and fittings.

- Costs of agents for letting and collecting rents.

- Insurance, including insurance premium tax.

- Interest payable on a loan to purchase, or improve, investment property (but see page 89 for restrictions).

- Charges for preparing inventories.

- Legal fees on renewing a tenancy agreement, for leases of not more than 50 years, or on the initial grant of a lease not exceeding 21 years.

- Accountancy fees to prepare and agree your income.

- Costs of collecting rents, which could in some cases include your travelling expenses to and from the property.

- Costs of services such as porters, cleaners, security.

- Wear and tear allowance for furniture and fittings: generally 10 per cent of the basic rent receivable. As an alternative, the cost of renewals may be claimed.

- Council tax.

Rent-a-room relief

Owner-occupiers and tenants who let furnished accommodation in their own or main home are able to receive rent up to £4,250 a year exempt from income tax. Make sure you tell your insurers and your mortgage company if you enter into a rent-a-room arrangement.

If rent exceeds these limits, you have the option of either paying tax on the excess without any deduction for allowable expenses, or calculating any profit made (gross rents less actual allowable expenses) and paying tax on that profit in the normal way.

An individual's exempt limit is halved if, at any time during a tax year, someone else received income from letting in the same property.

Income from trusts and settlements, etc.

Normally most estates of deceased persons will have a professional executor or administrator. They should provide you with a form R185, which will identify payments made to you, the rate of tax deducted and the type of trust. If you do not receive this form, then seek advice as to the details you need to include in your tax return.

Income from 'bare' trusts is considered as your own income as you effectively have control, and any income should be shown in the main tax return or relevant supplementary pages.

The tax return has supplementary pages covering Trusts, etc. (see page 52).

You may be able to claim tax back (see page 107) in respect of income from discretionary trusts if you are not a higher-rate taxpayer. In these supplementary pages you also have to give details of settlements made, for although capital or income may not have been received by you, it may be considered by the tax office to be your income for tax purposes. The most common example would be income from gifts you may have made to minor children.

Children's income

If you have made gifts of capital to your children who are under the age of 18, the total income resulting from the gifts should be included in your tax return as savings income if it is in excess of £100 gross (but *see also* page 153).

CHAPTER 8

Your 2011 tax return

Tax reliefs you can claim

This chapter covers payments made by you which may be allowed for tax relief and should be shown on your tax return. These could include interest charges on loans, covenants and donations to charities, maintenance payments, payments to tax-efficient investments, post-cessation expenses and payments to trade unions and friendly societies.

The relevant sections of the tax return are reproduced in Chapter 4.

Interest on loans for the purchase of private residence

There is no tax relief on interest on loans to buy a private residence.

Interest on other loans

There are other types of loans (called 'qualifying loans'), the interest on which is allowed for tax (see page 63).

They include loans to buy shares or lend to:

- A closely controlled trading company where you or a relative own more than 5 per cent of the company's shares or, if less, you have worked for the greater part of your time in the management of the company. Such interest is not allowed for tax if the shares qualified for tax relief under the business expansion scheme or enterprise investment scheme.

- A partnership.

- A co-operative, provided you work for it full time.

- An employee-controlled trading company (share acquisition only).

- Pay inheritance tax or buy plant or machinery for business use.

- An insurance company to buy an annuity if the person buying that annuity was aged 65 or over, the loan was secured on the individual's main residence in the UK or Republic of Ireland and the loan was taken out before 9 March 1999 (or other loans have replaced the original loan). Relief for these loans is restricted to the basic rate of tax up to a maximum loan of £30,000. You can request help sheet

IR340 for more information about what you can claim. You may also find the tax office helpline useful – telephone 0845 900 0444.

Interest paid on loans to buy an investment property

Property investments are assessed on the same basis as any other business (see page 121) – that is, the expenditure is allowable against profits if it is wholly and exclusively for business purposes.

Do not enter interest on a loan to buy an investment property in your main tax return; this has to be entered in the UK property supplementary pages (refer to page 45).

The interest rules also extend to overseas properties as well as those in the UK.

Retirement annuity payments and personal pensions

Refer to pages 163–167 for a summary of the tax-efficient opportunities that can arise from pension planning.

Hire purchase and credit card interest

You cannot claim relief on this type of interest unless you pay it in connection with your business activities.

Interest on overdue tax

This cannot be claimed as a deduction for tax purposes.

Maintenance and alimony payments

You can only get tax relief for maintenance and alimony payments if you, or your former husband, wife or civil partner, were born before 6 April 1935 and you make legally enforceable payments. The maximum relief that can be claimed is the lower of the actual maintenance payments made or £2,670 (£2,800 for 2011–2012) and relief is only given at 10 per cent. Such relief ceases if your former husband, wife or civil partner remarries.

Venture capital trusts and enterprise investment schemes

It is in the Reliefs section of the Additional information pages of your tax return that you need to state details of the investments. See page 162 for the tax advantages.

There is also a facility in this section to claim relief for any subscription to a community development finance institution (CDFI). State the amount you invested. Relief will be at 5 per cent per year of the amount you lend or invest for up to five years, or the amount that reduces your tax bill to zero for that year, if less.

Giving to charities under gift aid

The opportunities for giving to charities in a tax-efficient way have been considerably widened in the last few years. The sections of the tax return under which you can claim relief for giving to charity are shown on page 29. The five main options are: payroll giving schemes; covenants; cash donations under a gift aid scheme; the gifting of shares, securities, properties, etc. and donating your tax repayment directly to a charity.

Payroll giving schemes

Employers are allowed to run these schemes under which an employee can make donations to charity.

The donation is deducted from your pay and passed on to the charity by your employer. PAYE is calculated on your salary after making the deduction so that you are effectively getting immediate tax relief on the donation at your highest tax rate.

There is no need to mention this in your tax return as you will have declared your net earnings after the deduction has been made in the *Employment* supplementary pages.

Covenants to charities

Prior to 6 April 2000, covenants were used to transfer income in a tax-efficient way to charities; to be effective for income tax purposes they needed to be for more than three years.

You deducted tax from a payment under a deed of covenant at the basic rate and were able to get higher rate tax relief if applicable by claiming on your tax return.

Since the extension of the gift aid scheme there is no need for these types of covenant although existing covenants are still valid for tax relief.

Gifts of cash

This scheme applies to single gifts made by individuals and companies. There is no minimum limit for donations. Gifts are regarded as being made net of basic rate tax and charities are able to claim repayment of the tax. Relief is also available to non-residents who are liable to tax in the UK. Higher-rate tax relief can be claimed where applicable by filling in the appropriate boxes in your tax return (see page 29).

Most charities have gift aid declaration forms for you to complete when you make a donation that will enable them to reclaim the tax.

If you do not pay tax, you should not use gift aid, otherwise you will eventually have to reimburse the tax office for the basic rate tax deducted. The tax office publish a free booklet (IR65) on Giving to charity.

Carry-back and carry-forward relief

In the tax return in box 7 you can elect to have any gift aid payments made after 5 April 2010 backdated to the 2009–2010 tax year for tax relief purposes. Similarly, in box 8, you can treat any payments made between 5 April 2011 and the date you file your tax return (31 January 2012 at the latest) backdated to 2010–2011. It is up to you, not the tax office, to decide whether you wish to do this – obviously you would only do so if it saved you tax, as it will do in the vast majority of cases.

Gifts of shares, securities, land and buildings

You can gift quoted shares and securities to charities and the full market value of the gift as well as the costs of transfer can be offset against your taxable income.

Similarly you can gift land and buildings to charities. Individuals should enter the amount in boxes 9 or 10 of their tax return. There is no limit to the value of the gift, and in addition to income tax relief, the share sale or transfer to the charity will be free of capital gains tax.

If you are contemplating making a gift of shares or property to a charity and you are already making a profit on them, then it would be more tax efficient if you gave the assets directly to the charity rather than selling them first. It would also benefit the charity more, tax-wise.

With effect from April 2012 the inheritance tax rate will be cut from 40 per cent to 36 per cent if at least 10 per cent of your estate is left to charity (see Chapter 16).

Donating your tax repayment to charity

If you are due a tax repayment then you can nominate that all, or part, of it is paid directly to a charity of your choice. You need to complete the form *Giving your tax repayment to charity* which you will find in your tax return pack. If you don't know the charity number, then telephone the helpline on 0845 9000 444.

Trade annuities and patent royalties

If you made these payments for genuine commercial reasons in connection with your trade or profession, then box 4 of the *Additional information* pages of your tax return enables you to claim additional relief if you are a higher-rate taxpayer as they will have been treated as having been made after basic rate tax has been deducted.

Payments to trade unions and friendly societies

If you make compulsory payments to provide annuities for a widow or orphan where relief is not given by your employer, or if part of your trade union subscription relates to a pension, insurance or funeral benefit, or you have a friendly society policy providing sickness and death benefits, then you can claim tax relief on one half of the payments in box 8 in the *Additional information* pages (see page 63).

CHAPTER 9

Personal tax allowances and tax credits

A tax allowance is not a payment; it is the amount of income you can receive without paying tax. Apart from the personal allowance, all allowances are claimed by filling in a tax return. The allowances for 2011–2012 as announced in the budget are as follows (for allowances for previous years see page 186).

Personal allowance

From the moment that someone is born, they are entitled to a basic personal tax allowance each year.

Age as at 6 April 2011	£
Under 65	7,475
Between 65 and 74*	9,940
75 and over*	10,090

Notes
From April 2011, this personal allowance will be gradually withdrawn for income over £100,000, regardless of age, at a rate of £1 of allowance lost for every £2 over £100,000.
*These age-related allowances are restricted if your income is over £24,000. For every £2 of income above this limit, your allowance is reduced by £1, but no taxpayer can get less than the basic personal allowance of £7,475 unless their income is over £100,000 (see above).

The personal allowance for the under 65s will be increased to £8,105 from April 2012.

The married couple's allowance

The term 'married couple' also applies to same-sex couples who have registered their relationship in a civil partnership since 5 December 2005; therefore such couples can claim the same tax allowances as a married couple.

The married couple's allowance was abolished from 6 April 2000 except for couples where either the husband or wife was born before 6 April 1935 or where one person born before this date has married on or after 6 April 2000. The allowance for 2011–2012 is £7,295 for those aged 75 and over.

Relief is restricted to 10 per cent and the allowance is reduced, depending on your income level, by £1 for every £2 that your income exceeds the income limit of £24,000, but it cannot be reduced below the minimum amount of £2,800.

The personal allowance income restriction (see above) is applied before restricting the married couple's allowance.

In a heterosexual marriage, the wife can claim one half of the married couple's allowance, or indeed the whole allowance, if her husband agrees. Ask your tax office for form 18, but this has to be submitted before the start of the tax year to which it relates.

If it is preferred that the husband gets the whole of the married couple's allowance then there is no need to take any action.

In the case of civil partnerships, the allowance will initally go to the partner with the highest income, but again a request can be made to transfer one half, or the whole allowance, between partners.

Blind person's allowance

A registered blind person is entitled to an extra tax allowance of £1,980 (£1,890 for 2010–2011). This is also claimable by blind persons in the year preceding the year in which they were officially registered blind if, at the end of the previous year, evidence was available to support the eventual registration. The allowance is transferable to a husband or wife, or between civil partners, even if he or she is not blind.

Child tax credit (CTC)

This is a payment that is made by HMRC to help support families with children. It started in April 2003 and is made up of various elements as detailed in Appendix 4 on page 184.

You can claim for each child or young person up to 1 September following their 16th birthday (and up to age 20 if they are in full-time education) if you are responsible for looking after them. You do not have to be in paid employment to claim it. Claiming the child tax credit does not affect your entitlement to child benefit which, like the child tax credit, is not taxable and does not have to be declared on your tax return.

In spite of its name, the child tax credit will be paid directly to the responsible person and not through the tax system.

The chart reproduced in Appendix 4 shows the figures for 2010–2011 and those announced for 2011–2012.

Is it means tested?
Yes it is, but you can have joint income of at least £41,300 a year before you lose the benefit, so the earnings levels are quite generous.

What income is considered?
If you are single (or separated), your claim will be based on your income; if you are a married couple, or a man and a woman living together as if you are married, or in a civil partnership, then your combined total income will be taken into account.

Total income is considered to include earnings from employment or self-employment, some social security benefits, income from taxable savings and investments including rents (but excluding rent-a-room income). You are, however, allowed to deduct payments into a pension scheme and donations to gift aid before the credit is calculated; the calculation also ignores the first £300 of any pension income, property or investment income or foreign income.

If your circumstances change
Your income levels for the previous tax year (up to 5 April) should have been used for assessing any 2011 entitlement. If a change occurs in your circumstances – for example, your earnings take you into a higher band, or you have further children, you change jobs or your marital status changes – you must tell the tax office, either by filling in form TC602 or by telephoning the helpline 0845 300 3900 (0845 603 2000 in Northern Ireland). If you do not advise of changed circumstances then you may have to repay any tax credit overpayments.

If you are due extra child tax credit it will only be backdated for three months, so remain vigilant.

Once your annual income exceeds the limits for child tax credit or working tax credit (see below), the sequence in which you start to lose credits is: firstly the basic working tax credit is withdrawn, then any childcare element and finally the child element of the child tax credit is lost.

Once the upper earnings limit is reached, you lose the family element of the child tax credit.

Further information
For further information, telephone the claim line on 0845 300 3900. There is also a do-it-yourself calculator on the tax credits website **www.direct.gov.uk**, which will give you a better idea of whether it is worth claiming.

In addition to the child tax credit you may also be eligible for the working tax credit.

Working tax credit (WTC)

This is a payment to top up the earnings of those who are in low-income employment. Generally speaking, if you do not have children, you can earn £12,900 a year if you are single, and £17,700 if you are a couple before WTC is withdrawn. The amount you will receive will depend on your income level, the number of hours you work, your age, whether you have any children for whom you are caring and whether you are involved in paying for childcare to a registered provider. The calculation is very complicated but Appendix 4 gives a broad idea of likely benefit levels (see page 184).

Any childcare element is paid directly to the person responsible for paying for that care. If you are self-employed, the WTC claim will be paid to you directly.

The telephone helpline and claim line for more information are the same as for the child tax credit above: 0845 300 3900.

As with the child tax credit, you must keep the tax office informed of any change in circumstances otherwise you will either not get all the tax credit to which you are entitled or you may have to repay sums where you have claimed too much.

The working tax credit is not taxable.

Overpayment

If the tax authorities have overpaid your working tax credit or child tax credit and it is not your fault, then if you can prove that was so, you do not have to repay any overpayment. Ask for Form TC846 to establish this claim. The tax authorities will not normally ask for repayment of your entitlement if the increase in your annual income between your declared income and actual income for the previous year is no greater than £10,000.

Annual review of tax credits

You will be sent a review form each year between April and June so that you can update your personal data, your income declaration and a request to review your claim. Do this promptly as there are strict time limits for each award period and these will be shown on your form.

Pension credit

The pension credit is designed to top up the weekly income of people aged 60 or over to a guaranteed minimum level.

This pension credit, which is means tested and which is administered by the Pension Service (a section of the Department for Work and Pensions), is made up of two parts, the guarantee credit and a savings credit.

The guarantee credit
This applies to anyone who is 60 or over and whose income is less than £137.35 a week (£132.60 for 2010–2011) for a single person and £209.70 (£202.40 for 2010–2011) for a couple (it is the age of the older partner that counts for this credit). *The pension credit will top up your income to these amounts.* The qualifying age is gradually being increased with the State pension age.

If you are a couple, your combined income is taken into account. The term 'couple' not only means a husband and wife and civil partners, but also encompasses a person with whom you live 'as if you are married to them' (this is the wording in the tax legislation).

You may get more credit if you are severely disabled, looking after a person who is severely disabled, or you have commitments to certain housing costs (for example, mortgage interest payments).

The savings credit
This is only applicable to those aged 65 or over. For a couple, at least one person must have reached the age of 65.

Under this part of the pension credit, you get extra money if you have income from savings where your savings exceed £10,000 – there are higher limits if you are in a care home. Savings (or capital as the legislation calls it) excludes the value of your own house, personal possessions and life policy surrender values but does include tax-exempt savings accounts (such as ISAs).

The fact that you may be living with your grown-up family does not mean that you cannot claim the pension credit – the claim is based on your income only; also, the fact that you own your own house does not mean that you cannot apply for the credit.

How to claim
You do not have to fill in complicated forms, which is just as well because to do the calculations yourself would need another book of explanations, as the formulae used for both parts of the pension credit calculation are unbelievably complicated.

To claim, telephone the Pension Service on 0800 99 1234 (0808 601 8821 in Northern Ireland). The text phone number is 0800 1690 133.

They will fill in the form for you and send the completed form to you for signature. You will need to tell them your national insurance number, your bank and savings details, and the amounts of any other pension you receive in addition to the State pension. They will also ask you for details of your housing costs. You will need to tell them into which account you would like your pension credit paid.

You can request a blank application form to fill in yourself if you don't want to get involved in a long telephone conversation, or you can download it from **www.thepensionservice.gov.uk/pensioncredit**.

If you have forgotten to claim, then you can get your application backdated for up to three months. The pension credit is not taxable.

The credit is paid weekly in advance directly into your bank, building society or post office account. If you have difficulty due to a mental or physical disability, it can be paid to you by cheque.

Re-assessment

You don't have to go through this claims procedure every year. Once your income is assessed at retirement, it is normally re-assessed every five years but you should notify the Pensions Service if your circumstances change materially, for example, you have married or divorced, moved house, or you have a significant change in earnings compared with when you first registered or you started to receive social security benefits.

If you disagree with any decision concerning your pension credit, then you should ask for it to be reviewed, but don't delay for too long for most re-assessments have very strict time limits – often within one month of the original notification.

CHAPTER 10

PAYE and tax codes

The Pay As You Earn system was introduced to enable every employee to pay tax by instalments rather than in one hefty amount at the end of the tax year. By law, your employer has to deduct PAYE tax and national insurance from your earnings.

How does an employer know how much to deduct?

You are allocated a tax code by your tax office, and that tells your employer how much you can earn before you start to pay tax. The code is a shortened method of defining your total tax-free pay (usually the total of your allowances), but in fact the last figure is omitted. The code effectively spreads your allowances evenly throughout the tax year. For example, a code 647L means that you start paying tax after you have earned £6,475 (£124.51 each week).

A PAYE coding notice is sent to you if your code changes; it details your allowances, benefits, untaxed income, etc., and shows your tax code. If you do not receive one, you can request a copy from your tax office. You will need to quote your tax reference and national insurance number.

Your employer is also advised of the new tax code but he is not given the details as to how it is compiled so he cannot check it for you.

You should make sure that all allowances due to you are included and be sure your code is amended if your allowances alter during the year.

The higher your tax code, the lower your tax, unless you have a tax code with a K prefix.

What do the letters mean?

The letter shown after your tax code defines your status. For example, L = basic personal allowance; P = full personal allowance if aged 65–74, with V being used if you are also entitled to the married couple's allowance and you are on basic rate tax; Y = personal allowance for those aged 75 or over. T is used if there are other items the tax office need to review, or if you have requested that you do not want the identification letter mentioned above to be used.

PAYE AND TAX CODES

Codes BR, DO or DI are sometimes used where you have more than one employer or have several sources of income and will mean that you will have tax deducted at basic or higher rates of tax. In these cases it is important to check your tax at the year end as there is a danger that you will have overpaid tax and need to claim a refund.

If you do have more than one employment, you can ask the tax office to apportion your personal allowance between the two and your PAYE code number will be altered accordingly.

Sometimes your taxable benefits will exceed your allowances – for example, if you are taxed on car and fuel benefits or private health benefits, or have arrears of tax to collect. In these cases a K code is used so that your employer can recoup this tax on behalf of the tax office.

The tax office may estimate any likely taxable benefits for the 2011–2012 tax year and will probably base them on the latest available figures on their files, which could be quite old if you haven't sent in a tax return for the last couple of years.

HMRC have admitted that a significant number of code numbers are wrong this year due to computer and administrative errors, so you need to check the figures on your PAYE coding notice carefully. If the estimates are excessive, write to your tax office requesting a code change – be sure to quote your NI number and the tax reference.

Emergency coding

If your employer does not know what tax code to use he will apply an 'emergency' code 747L for 2011–2012; this effectively only gives you the basic personal allowance (regardless of your age) and unless this is your first job the tax system will assume you started work in April, so that you could lose out on any tax-free pay due to you. The quicker you sort out your correct code number, the sooner you will have the correct tax deducted from your earnings.

How to check your tax code

Nowadays a PAYE coding notice comes in the form of a letter from HMRC and it will explain how your tax code is calculated.

It will certainly start by stating your personal allowance (and, if applicable, the blind person's allowance), to which will be *added* any gift aid payments if you are a higher-rate taxpayer, any allowable expenses, any pension payments which have not already had tax relief at the correct rate, and any married couple's allowance or maintenance allowance, although relief on these will be restricted to 10 per cent.

There will be *deductions* for any State pension or taxable State benefits you receive which will have been paid gross, and any benefits you have received from your employer, which will have been detailed in your P11D form, and any casual earnings that you have declared.

Tax underpayments that you had requested in your tax return should be collected via your PAYE code will be taken into account and shown separately.

Ideally, the figures making up your tax code should equate with the figures in your tax return. If they do not, then tell the tax office immediately, otherwise you could end up paying too little or too much tax for the rest of the year.

If your tax code is incorrect, it is more than likely that your previous year's code was also wrong, so that any overpayment of tax is accumulating.

Pay particular attention to any company car and fuel benefits, because following the introduction of new rules, many coding notices have again been issued showing incorrect benefits resulting in unwelcome tax demands at a later date.

Pensioners will often have a tax code applied to any supplementary pension they receive (see Chapter 12 on page 110).

CHAPTER 11

How to check your tax

At the end of the tax year you should check to see if you have paid the correct amount of tax. If you are self-employed you may need to keep a closer eye on your tax affairs during the year and Chapter 13 deals specifically with this.

This chapter is primarily for employees on PAYE, although it will be of interest to all taxpayers as many of the circumstances are not confined just to those on PAYE.

At the end of every tax year, your employer must give you a form P60, which will show how much you have earned in the tax year and, more importantly, how much tax you have paid.

If you receive employee benefits (company car, health insurance, etc.) you will also receive a form P11D (see page 72), which will identify these.

You should check for yourself whether the amount of tax you have paid is correct. This will mean that you need to add up all your income and benefits, deducting allowable expenses (see Chapter 6 on page 80) and any tax allowances, and calculating the tax payable.

If this total tax figure is less than that stated on your P60 form, then you have paid too much tax. Write immediately to your tax office pointing this out and then claim a refund. If you have not paid enough tax, either you or the tax inspector has made a mistake! If you have paid insufficient tax, you are under a legal obligation to send in a tax return so that any outstanding tax can be calculated and paid. The tax office may also adjust your code number so that you do not underpay tax in the following year.

There is a comprehensive chart you can use in the *Check Your Tax* calculator on pages 169–172, but on the next few pages there are simplified examples of how to check your own tax.

In the first example overleaf, Michael is a married man under 65 and the tax calculations are fairly straightforward as he has no savings income or dividends and his income does not take him into the higher rate tax band.

Assuming that these are the figures Michael declared in his 2011 tax return, then the statement he gets from the tax office should agree with his tax calculations and will also confirm that a refund is due.

• 103 •

If he had adjustments in his tax code to collect underpayments for earlier tax years, then these would need to be taken into the following calculation.

Example 1: Checking your tax for the year ended 5 April 2011

Michael, who is married and under 65, is employed and had a salary of £27,300 from which his employer had deducted a pension contribution of £750. His employer provided him with a company car and fuel. He did some freelance work at home which, after expenses, gave him £835. He also claimed £115 for professional subscriptions. His tax liability can be summarised as follows:

	£	£
Total wages per P60 form	27,300	
Less: Pension contribution	750	26,550
Casual earnings		835
Use of company car and fuel benefit, say		5,500
Total earnings for the year		32,885
Less: Expenses claimed		115
Net earnings		32,770
Less: Personal allowance		6,475
Total income on which tax is payable		26,295
Tax payable £26,295 at 20 per cent		5,259
Less: Tax paid under PAYE as shown on P6 form, say		5,400
Amount of tax to be claimed back		£ 141

The tax office uses a different method

The way in which the above statement was prepared is the normal and simplest way, and the method most accountants would use. Unfortunately, our tax system always makes things as complicated as possible and the statements you receive from the tax office will present the details in a different format. They tend to work backwards, allocating income against tax bands.

However, the net result should be the same and if it is not and you cannot see why there is a difference, write to your tax office and enclose a copy of your workings so they can identify the problems.

Tax on savings income

For 2010–2011 there was a starting income tax rate of 10 per cent on savings income only (excluding dividends), so that if your non-savings income, after allowances, was less than £2,440 then you paid tax at only 10 per cent on savings income within that £2,440 band.

There are higher figures for 2011–2012 (see page 186).

Tax on dividends

Just to complicate matters further, dividend income is paid after deducting a tax credit of 10 per cent. Add this credit to the dividend received to give the gross amount to be included in your total income.

For basic rate taxpayers this tax credit covers their tax liability on dividend income, but higher-rate taxpayers will be taxed at 32.5 per cent or 42.5 per cent. Dividend income is treated as the top slice of your savings income (see page 186).

This tax credit cannot be reclaimed if you are a non-taxpayer, nor has it been repayable since 6 April 2004 on shares held in personal equity plans (PEPs) and individual savings accounts (ISAs). Therefore, if you are a non-taxpayer, choose investments that pay interest without tax having been deducted before you receive it (see Chapter 18).

Checking your tax

As you will see, the tax system is unnecessarily complicated, but it can be made much simpler to understand if you remember to use the *Check Your Tax* sequence list.

The *Check Your Tax* sequence list

This is the easy way to calculate your tax for 2010–2011. It is vital that you do your calculations in the following order:

1. Make a list of your total income under the following headings:

2. **Non savings income and benefits.** Deduct from this income your net personal tax allowances after restrictions, allowable expenses, and pension payments. The balance is taxed at 20 per cent until the limit of £37,400 is reached. Any excess over this figure is taxed at 40 per cent, and at 50 per cent over £150,000.

3. **Non-dividend savings income.** If your income excluding any non-dividend savings income but after allowances (as above) is less than £2,440 then you will pay tax at only 10 per cent on any savings income within the £2,440 band. However if non-savings income exceeds the starting rate limit for savings (£2,440), the 10 per cent savings rate is not available.

4. **Dividend income.** Taxed at 10 per cent until the limit of the cumulative 20 percent band is reached (£37,400). Any excess over this figure is taxed at 32.5 per cent or 42.5 per cent (see page 186).

5. **Capital gains tax.** Net capital gains are taxable at either 18 per cent or 28 per cent depending on your income level (see page 138).

Further examples

On page 104 it was explained how Michael, who had a straightforward income structure without any savings income, calculated his tax.

Here are two more examples: Jane, who is a basic rate taxpayer but has savings income; and Alan who is a higher-rate taxpayer with savings income and dividends and who also made a gift aid donation during the year.

Example 2: Checking your tax for the year ended 5 April 2011

In 2010–2011 Jane has a total income after allowances of £5,360, which includes £500 interest *received gross*.

Jane will pay tax at 20 per cent on all her income because her non-savings income after allowances is higher than £2,440. She will not be eligible for the savings rate tax band.

	£		£
	4,860	at the basic rate of 20 per cent	972
	500	at the basic rate of 20 per cent	100
Total income	£ 5,360	Tax payable	£ 1,072

If Jane had received interest net after tax had been deducted, then the total income would still remain the same, for you must always include the gross amount of any income, but the amount of tax payable would be: £972 less £100 (20 per cent × £500) being tax already deducted from the interest.

Example 3: Checking your tax for the year ended 5 April 2011

Alan is married and under 65; he has a salary of £42,500, makes a pension contribution and receives benefits from his employer. He also has casual earnings, interest from a building society and dividends from shares. He also gave £500 to a local charity and signed a gift aid form so, as he is a higher-rate taxpayer, he can claim the difference between the basic and higher rate tax rate. This is how Alan would go about checking his tax liability.

Alan lists his total income, less expenses and allowances, as follows:

	£	£
Total salary shown on his P60 form	42,500	
Less: Pension contribution	3,800	38,700
Casual earnings		695
Use of company car and fuel benefit, say		5,500
Total earnings for the year		44,895
Less: Expenses claimed		215
Net earnings		44,680
Less: Personal allowance		6,475
Non-savings income		38,205
Non-dividend savings income received	432	
Tax deducted at 20 per cent	108	540
Dividend income received	450	
Tax credit	50	500
Total income		£39,245

As this total is above the maximum 20 per cent basic rate band of £37,400, Alan is going to be a higher-rate taxpayer. Therefore apply the sequence as shown on the previous page to calculate his tax liability as follows.

		£		£
Tax on his non-savings income:		37,400	at 20 per cent	7,480
£38,205–£37,400		805	at 40 per cent	322
Non-savings income total		38,205		
Tax on his non-dividend savings income:				
the 20 per cent band has been fully used above therefore:		£540	at 40 per cent	216
Tax on his dividend income:				
the 20 per cent band has been fully used above therefore:		£500	at 32.5 per cent	162
				£8,180
Less: claim for gift aid donation				
Gross amount £625 (£500 × $\frac{100}{80}$) at 20 per cent (40%–20%)				125
				£8,055

Alan will already have paid much of this by PAYE deducted from his salary (let's say this was £7,750) and has paid tax by deduction on his interest and dividend income.

So, Alan's final tax bill will be:

Tax liability as above		8,055
Less: Paid under PAYE	£7,750	
Deducted from interest	108	
Tax credit on dividend	50	7,908
Further tax demand to pay		£ 147

Income tax repayment claim

If most of the income you receive has already been taxed (for example, interest) it is possible that you can claim back some tax.

Either fill in a self assessment tax return if you have received one or ask for a repayment claim form (form R40), telling your tax office in a covering letter that you think you are due a tax refund.

On form R40 you can claim expenses and deductions in the same way as an ordinary tax return. You do not have to send dividend vouchers and certificates of deduction of tax in support of your claim. However, you should still keep the records as you may be asked to produce evidence at a later date.

Do not forget, when you sign the declaration, that there is another part of the form that you need to sign, which is your legal request for the actual repayment of tax to be made to you.

The following example shows how Joan is due a tax refund and the way it is calculated.

Example 4: Tax repayment for the year 2010–2011

Joan, who is under 65, had a part-time job and earned £4,500, from which tax has not been deducted at source. She also received net interest from a building society of £2,000 (tax deducted £500).

	£	£
Non-savings income		4,500.00
Interest received (building society)	2,000	
Tax deducted (i.e. 20 per cent of £2,500)	500	2,500.00
Total income		7,000.00
Deduct personal allowance		6,475.00
Net income		525.00

Joan's personal allowance is used first against her earnings of £4,500. Therefore, all her remaining taxable income is savings income. Her tax liability is therefore:

Tax liability: £525 at 10 per cent	52.50
Less: tax deducted from interest	500.00
Tax refund due	£ 447.50

If Joan had received net *dividend* income of £2,000, instead of building society interest, she would not have been able to reclaim the tax credit that would have been deducted from her dividend.

Tax demands in respect of 2010–2011 income

If your only income is taxed under PAYE, then it is unlikely that you will receive a tax return to complete and, provided you have checked that the right amount of tax had been deducted and your current PAYE tax code is correct, then there is no need to contact your tax office.

If you have other income, or gains, in the year ended 5 April 2011 then you probably need to fill in a tax return. You should complete this and return it to your tax office before 31 October 2011. If you file electronically you have until 31 January 2012.

The tax office will then send you a self assessment tax calculation (form SA 302) showing any sums due (or overpaid).

Tax payments

Unless you are self-employed, or have sources of untaxed income, most of your tax liability will be paid by PAYE, or by deductions at source, throughout the year; when you send in your tax return, any tax due will be accounted for at the tax year end and is payable by 31 January of the following year.

If you are self-employed, however, or you have income or interest that has not been taxed or you are a higher-rate taxpayer with investment income, you may still have to make two payments on account (see page 33).

From time to time your tax office might send you self assessment statements (form SA300) showing you the current position of your tax payments (or refunds). If it is correct, then any tax due must be paid by the date shown; if you disagree with the amount, ask for form SA303 on which you can claim to reduce any payments on account, or write giving your explanation why you think the figures are wrong. You must still pay any tax that you think is due, however, otherwise interest will be charged.

Interest on late payments and repayments

The tax office will charge you interest on underpayments from the due date but they will pay you interest on overpayments. This is called a repayment supplement and it is not taxable. The interest rate for repayment supplements is currently much lower than the interest rate on underpayments, somewhat unfairly.

CHAPTER 12

Pensioners

This chapter applies primarily to those people who have reached the State pension age of 65 for men and 60 for women. If you have elected for an earlier retirement you continue to be treated as a taxable individual and you cannot claim the tax concessions available to pensioners until the official retirement age. A married man is entitled to claim the State retirement pension when he reaches 65. On the other hand, if a married woman reaches 60 before her husband is 65, she can only claim the pension if she has paid sufficient national insurance contributions in her own right.

The State retirement pension age for women is to be increased to 65 by November 2018 and will then increase to 66 for both men and women by April 2020.

Shortly before you reach retirement age you should receive form P161 from your tax office. Fill this in and return it to ensure that you get the correct age allowance and the correct tax code is eventually applied to any pension income you will receive, other than the State pension.

Telephone the Pension Service on 0800 731 7898 if you are two months from retirement and have not had a letter advising you of your pension entitlements. There is also a useful website on **www.the pensionservice.gov.uk**.

If the State pension is going to be your only income then you can apply to your local Department for Work and Pensions office and local council for various benefits to supplement your income; and also consider claiming tax credits (see page 97).

What to do when you retire

If you have been paying PAYE, you will receive a form P45 from your employer. Send this to the tax office printed on the form, with a letter stating that you have retired, giving the date on which you reached retirement age, details of any pensions you will receive, and stating that you are not intending to take further employment.

Should you later decide to work again, either full time or part time, you will have to ask your tax office for a new tax code.

If you have been self-employed, make sure that your tax returns are up to date and tax liabilities agreed, and inform your tax office of the details of any private pension you will receive.

Pensions

The State pension, the SERPS supplement and the widow's pension, are taxable, but the Government does not deduct the tax when you receive or collect them. If this State pension is your only source of income, however, then it is unlikely that you will have any tax to pay as your personal allowance will more than cover this income. The war widow's pension is not taxable, neither is the winter fuel payment or cold weather payments, nor the state Christmas bonus.

Postponing your State pension

You can delay taking your State pension for as long as you wish and get either an extra payment added to your pension for each year of postponement, or a lump sum.

Why would you want to postpone? If you have enough income to live on at the moment, then receiving the State pension may put you into a higher tax bracket and it would be beneficial to delay taking that extra income until perhaps your other income is at a lower level.

You have three options available as regards your State pension entitlements once you reach official retirement age.

1. You can retire and claim your State pension.

2. You can carry on working and claim your State pension.

3. You can delay claiming your State pension – whether you are working or not.

If you decide to delay claiming, you have a further two options to consider:

4. You can earn extra State pension that will be added to your normal entitlement when you do decide to claim; the extra amount will be equivalent to 1 per cent of your weekly pension for every five weeks you put off claiming.

or

5. You can claim a one-off lump sum payment based on the amount of State pension you would have received in the period you have put off claiming plus interest; this interest rate will be 2 per cent above the Bank of England's base rate.

You can only opt for the lump sum option if you put off claiming for at least 12 consecutive months.

The phrase 'State pension' includes any earnings-related State pension (SERPS) or S2P (State second pension) and any graduated retirement benefit.

Tax position on lump sum payment

This lump sum payment needs to be added to your total income for tax purposes, and if this total exceeds your personal allowance you will pay tax on it.

However, the inclusion of any lump sum will only be taxed at the tax rate applicable to your other income; in other words, if you are in the 20 per cent band for 2010–2011 and the addition of a lump sum would take you into the 40 per cent band, the lump sum will only be taxable at 20 per cent.

The pension service will deduct tax from the lump sum payment – you will have to fill in a form stating what you think your total income will be for the year so they can decide what rate of tax to deduct.

Any lump sum will not affect your entitlement to the age-related personal tax allowance. The lump sum will be excluded from your savings total when calculating any savings-credit part of the pension credit.

Even if you are already receiving the State pension you can elect to stop receiving it and adopt one of the above options.

The pension service has published a booklet, *Your State pension choice – Pension now or extra pension later. A guide to State pension deferral.* Telephone 0845 7313 233 for a copy.

Working after retirement

If you carry on working after the official retirement age you can still claim the State pension, although you do not have to pay any more national insurance contributions (employers still have to contribute, however).

Whether you are employed full time or part time, a PAYE tax code will be issued (see Chapter 10) that will tax your earnings.

Pension credit

This pension credit is designed to top up pensioners' income, whilst at the same time rewarding (slightly) those who had saved for their retirement. This replaced the minimum income guarantee. See page 97 for full details to see if you can benefit from making a claim.

Tax allowances

A husband, wife or civil partner each has their own tax allowance and is responsible for their own tax affairs.

The tax allowances for 2011–2012 for those aged 65 or over are as follows with the 2010–2011 figures in brackets:

Tax allowances for 2011–2012		
Age for personal allowance	*Personal allowance* £	*Married couple's allowance* £
65–74	9,940 (9,490)	–
75 and over	10,090 (9,640)	7,295 (6,965)

Notes
You get this personal allowance for a whole year for anyone who is 65 and over (or 75 and over) at any time during the tax year.
Although the married couple's allowance was abolished from 6 April 2000, it still continues for those couples where either the husband or wife or civil partner was aged 65 or more on or before 5 April 2000 and is based on the age of the *older* of the husband or wife or partner. Relief is restricted to only 10 per cent of the allowance.

However, these age-related personal allowances, as they are called, are reduced if your own total income is above £24,000. For every £2 of income above this limit, your allowance is reduced by £1, but no taxpayer can get less than the basic personal allowance of £7,475 unless your income is above £100,000, in which case the personal allowance is gradually withdrawn at the rate of £1 of allowance lost for every £2 over £100,000. The married couple's allowance will be reduced by the excess that has not already been taken into account in calculating the reduced personal allowance. The allowance cannot be reduced below a minimum level – £2,800 for 2011–2012 and £2,670 for 2010– 2011.

Don't forget that a wife's income from all sources is considered separately from that of her husband, and similarly for civil partners.

How to check your tax for 2010–2011

Start by working out your total income for the year. You must include all your pension income, including the State pension and the gross amount of any interest from banks, building societies, annuities, etc. Also include any dividend income, including the tax credit. You do not have to include any income that is free of tax (see page 13).

Secondly, you need to make a note of any tax that you have already had deducted from your pension or other income. Finally you need to calculate any allowances to which you are entitled.

Example of how to check your tax for 2010–2011

John, the husband, is aged 76 and his wife, Mary, is 69.

	John £	Mary £
Income for 2010–2011		
State pension, say	8,500	2,850
Other pension, gross amount (tax deducted, say £1,500)	8,886	
Rent from letting unfurnished room (after expenses)	4,046	
Total non-savings income	21,432	2,850
National Saving Bank interest:		
Ordinary account £40 (the first £70 is not taxable)	–	
Investment account (gross)	–	75
Bank deposit interest – received £ 144		
Tax deducted before receipt 36	180	
Dividend income – received 1,800		
– tax credit 200	2,000	
Total income	23,612	2,925
Less: Personal allowance 9,640		9,490
but restricted because of		(6,565)
John's income limit (see note)		unused
£23,612–£22,900 = £712		allowance
× 50 per cent 356	9,284	
Taxable income	£14,328	

Now refer to the easy way sequence list on page 105 so that you use the correct percentages in calculating your tax.

John's tax liability will be:		£
On his non-savings income £21,432		
Less: his allowances £ 9,284 = £12,148		
£12,148 at 20 per cent		2,429
On his savings income £180 at 20 per cent		36
On his dividend income £2,000 at 10 per cent		200
14,328		2,665
Less: married couple's allowance £6,965 at 10 per cent		696
Total tax liability		1,969
But he has already paid by deduction the following amounts of tax:		
On his other pension £1,500		
On his bank interest 36		
On his dividends 200		1,736
Tax still to pay		£ 233

Notes

1. John's total income was £23,612; as the income age limit is £22,900 his allowances are reduced by 50 per cent (£1 for every £2 over this limit). This could have been avoided if some of his income-producing assets had been transferred to Mary, his wife.

2. It will be seen that Mary had insufficient income to cover her personal allowance. The unused balance is lost – it cannot be used by her husband. It would have been more sensible for her to have received a greater part of the family income in order to reduce John's tax liability, so they should consider reorganising their investments to avoid the same problem arising next year.

3. Perhaps John should also have let the room furnished instead of unfurnished, with the lodger sharing the house so that the rent could have been received tax free under the rent-a-room scheme (see page 87).

4. As John's non-savings income after his personal allowance is more than £2,440, he is not entitled to the 10 per cent savings rate.

Remember that if a situation arises where a husband is unable to use part of his married couple's allowance, the balance can be transferred to his wife – ask for Form 575 from your tax office. Similarly with civil partnerships. You have up to five years from 31 January following the tax year in which to make this request.

As mentioned in the notes in the table, John could save tax by transferring some income-bearing investments to his wife, but she should not receive dividends as she cannot reclaim the tax credit if her income remains below her personal allowance; investments paying interest tax free would be preferable (see Chapter 18).

Income tax repayment

At the end of each tax year on 5 April you should check to see exactly what income you received during the previous year and what tax you have actually paid, as in the above example.

You can get a repayment of tax if you have paid too much. To reclaim tax ask your tax office for leaflet IR110 and a form R40. Complete it in the same way as a tax return (see Chapter 4 on page 21) and send the form to your tax office. There is no need to enclose the dividend and interest vouchers unless the tax office ask for them at a later date.

Where most of your income has already had tax deducted before you receive it (for example, interest) you may be able to make quarterly, half-yearly or annual repayment claims (see page 107).

Even if you are a taxpayer, you may have had tax deducted from interest received at 20 per cent and because you may be entitled to the 10 per cent savings rate (see page 186) you should claim a refund of the difference. There are a great number of pensioners on low incomes who are not making these claims.

Where to invest your money

In reviewing investments, married and civil partner pensioners in particular should make sure that they are making full use of both personal allowances. They should avoid a situation arising where perhaps one partner is paying tax and the other partner is not using his or her full allowance. To correct such a problem, you should consider switching savings or investments from one to the other.

If you have insufficient income to cover your personal allowances (in other words, you are not a taxpayer) it is important to put your savings into investments that do not deduct tax before paying the interest. Otherwise you will only have to cope with more paperwork in claiming the tax back at the end of the year.

In Chapter 18 on page 158 there is a brief summary of the various investment alternatives that are available for savings depending on your circumstances and clarifying whether or not you have to pay tax on the interest or dividends received.

Building society and bank accounts

A special mention should be made here about these accounts. Many pensioners who may be on low incomes put their savings into building society or bank accounts for safety and convenience. However, tax will be deducted from the interest before you receive it and if you are not a taxpayer (that is, your personal tax allowances exceed your total income) then you should claim the tax back at the end of the year (see page 107). Many people, however, don't realise that they have to do this and consequently they are losing out. It is official knowledge that there are many millions of pounds in tax refunds that have not been claimed.

Your bank or building society will pay your interest gross, without deducting tax, if you ask them for a form R85. This is a very simple form to complete and asks you to certify that your total income for the tax year is unlikely to exceed your personal allowances. If you are aged 65 to 74 on 5 April 2011 these figures for 2011–2012 are £9,940; if you are aged 75 or more they are £10,819 for a married man or civil partner and £10,090 for single people (assuming an election has not been made to transfer all or part of the married couple's allowance).

You will need your national insurance number to complete this form. If your circumstances change during the tax year and your total income is such that you will become liable to tax, you must inform your bank or building society branch immediately.

Equity release schemes

With higher property prices, compared with say, a decade ago, thousands of pensioners appear to be fairly well off on paper, but in terms of income for everyday living expenses they find it hard to make ends meet. This is where equity release schemes come into play.

Under these schemes you sell all or part of your house for a discounted lump sum and continue to live in it. Or, instead of a lump sum, you can receive a regular income.

There are three main schemes: home reversion schemes, lifetime mortgages and home income plans.

With the first two schemes there are no income tax implications, although clearly the value of your estate, including your house, will reduce the longer the equity release scheme stays in place and this might reduce any inheritance tax liability; on the other side of the coin, you will be reducing the value of any inheritance that you may wish to pass on to children, relatives or friends when you die.

With these two schemes it is important that you approach several firms for quotations, use an independent solicitor (not one recommended by the scheme itself) and ensure that you have the greatest degree of flexibility if your circumstances change and you want to terminate the scheme or move house.

With home income plans, instead of receiving a lump sum as with the above schemes, you can elect to take an annuity in order to give you an ongoing income. (See below for the tax implications.)

Purchased life annuities

Do not confuse these with annuities you purchase with a pension fund. These are taxed quite differently.

When you receive a purchased annuity payment it consists of two elements: capital and income. The capital portion is non-taxable but the insurance company will deduct tax from the income portion (which you must enter on your tax return) and provide you with a tax deduction certificate, which you will need in order to claim any tax repayment. Tax will be deducted at the basic rate of 20 per cent. You will not get any tax relief on buying the actual annuity.

Annuities are particularly useful if you have no dependants or your children or relatives do not need additional assets.

Bear in mind that any extra income from an annuity could reduce any means-tested social security benefit, could affect your age-related personal allowance and will not take inflation into account in succeeding years. Also, you cannot cancel an annuity and get your capital back.

Pre-1999 annuity

Provided at least 90 per cent of the lump sum received on mortgaging your house was used to buy the annuity and the loan was taken out before 9 March 1999, then the interest on a mortgage of up to £30,000 will be tax deductible at the basic rate, even though mortgage interest tax relief was abolished for other loans from 6 April 2000. You had to be 65 or over at 9 March 1999.

Your pension scheme retirement options

If you are a member of your employer's pension scheme or have a personal pension scheme of your own, it is important to consider all the options when you retire. This is fully covered in Chapter 18 on page 166.

CHAPTER 13

Self-employed

A self-employed person is one who owns a business as a sole trader or is in partnership with someone else. If you trade as a limited company, you, as a director, are an employee and not self-employed, and the company is a separate legal entity, having its own tax return, and paying corporation tax.

Advantages of being self-employed

There are definite advantages in being self-employed as there are more opportunities for self-employed people to reduce their tax bill than an employed person. There are more expenses that can be claimed and they are somewhat easier to claim. In addition, there is loss relief which can be set against other taxable income or, in the early years of a business, can be carried back against your total income for the previous three years.

If you are self-employed, you may find it more convenient to deal with the paperwork and meet some of your business contacts at your home. This, in effect, becomes a second place of business, so that you can claim against your profits a proportion of your household expenses, such as heating and lighting.

Start off on the right lines

1. When you start a new business, you must tell your tax office within three months of starting, otherwise you could face a fine of £100.

2. You also need to notify the NI contributions office so that you do not build up arrears of NI contributions or miss out on benefits. The tax office issues a booklet *Starting your own business* CWL1, which has useful advice and a form which can be used to notify the relevant departments that you have started trading. There is a helpline for the newly self-employed on 0845 915 4515.

3. You might have a tax liability in the first year, unless you make a loss, or your profit is offset by allowances or reliefs. Do not wait for the tax office to send you a tax return – ask for one.

4. You may have been employed before starting up in business on your own. If so, you should send the P45 form you will have

received from your previous employer to your local tax office and you may be able to claim a tax refund immediately.

5. If you do not use your own name, you must show the names and addresses of the owners of the business on business letters, orders, invoices, receipts and demands for payment. You must also display the names and addresses at your business premises.

6. It may be advantageous to take your wife, husband or civil partner in as a business partner if they are not already employed elsewhere. However, it should be borne in mind that both partners become jointly and severally liable for the partnership debts, which might put family assets, including your house, in jeopardy. Also in the case of divorce, the business could be seriously affected. Do not forget that, depending on earnings levels and share of profits, there will be a liability for each partner to pay tax and national insurance contributions.

7. When you are in a partnership it is advisable to have a written agreement setting out its terms, particularly if your wife or husband is a partner.

8. You should open a separate bank account for your business which, in the case of a partnership, should be in the partnership names.

9. Keep books detailing your business dealings: the minimum you should keep are a cash book for all monies received and paid, an analysis book for purchases and one for sales, and a petty cash book for miscellaneous expenses. It is essential that you keep all purchase invoices and copy sales invoices, not only for the purpose of preparing your accounts but also to keep a check on the amounts you may have to pay and charge in respect of value added tax.

10. Check your turnover – should you register for VAT? The turnover limits above which you must register are £73,000 for 2011–2012 (£70,000 for 2010–2011). The de-registration limits are £71,000 and £68,000 respectively. The standard rate of VAT was cut to 15 per cent from 1 December 2008 and reverted to 17.5 per cent on 1 January 2010. It increased to 20 per cent from 4 January 2011. The reduced rate continued to remain at 5 per cent.

11. Always bear in mind that HMRC's tax inspectors have a legal right to require you to supply evidence from your books and records for any particular year both in terms of income tax and VAT. Under self assessment you must keep books and records for five years and ten months from the end of the tax year.

12. Make regular provision for a retirement pension (see page 163).

13. If you run your business from your own house then do bear in mind that there may be a capital gains tax liability (see page 141). Also check the council tax situation.

14. Check your insurances – advise your insurers if you are operating from your home address or using your own car for business.

15. Consider establishing a limited liability partnership (LLP), the main purpose of which is to protect partners from excessive legal claims against the partnership, which could jeopardise their personal assets.

16. During the current recession, HMRC are looking more sympathetically at businesses that are experiencing cash flow problems in paying their PAYE, NI or VAT on the due date and they will probably grant an extended payment schedule provided you contact them and explain your situation.

How are you taxed?

Many self-employed people think you pay tax only on what you take out of the business for yourself as drawings or wages. This is not so. Drawings are sums taken on account of the profit you expect to make. You are taxed on your total profit before deducting any drawings.

To find out how much profit you have made, prepare accounts showing your total business income less your business expenses. This is not necessarily the figure on which your tax is calculated, for you have to add any disallowable items mentioned below.

It is this amended profit figure, not the one shown in your accounts, that you should enter in your tax return. Your claim for capital allowances must also be entered (see page 125). This adjustment and claim for capital allowances is called a tax computation

Refer to the actual *Self-employed* supplementary tax return pages reproduced on page 40; also the *Partnership* pages on page 43.

Allowable expenses and deductions

Apart from your normal business expenses (such as the purchase of goods, rent, rates, staff wages) you should consider claiming the following:

- Hotel and travelling expenses on business trips – not forgetting part of the total running expenses of your car.
- The business usage part of your private telephone bill.
- Bank interest and charges on your business account.
- Business subscriptions and magazines.

- Special clothing necessary for your type of business, including cleaning costs, etc.
- Bad and doubtful debts that can be specifically identified.
- Gifts advertising your business (but the cost must not exceed £50 per person, and must not be for food, drink, tobacco or vouchers).
- Repairs and renewals to business property (for example, the cost of replacing a shopfront, less any part of that cost representing any improvement).
- Employer's national insurance contributions on employee's wages and benefits (see page 131 for your own NIC liability).

Expenses and deductions not allowable

It is possible that your business payments include some expenses which are not allowable for tax. In this case, your profit must be increased so as to exclude this private element. Examples of the more usual items are a proportion of:

- Rent, light, heat and council tax – where you live in part of the business premises (for example, a flat above your shop).
- Motor car expenses, including hire purchase interest, where you use a business car for private journeys.
- Telephone bills.

And the whole of:

- Depreciation on all assets, if included in your accounts, whether they are business or private. You can instead claim capital allowances (see page 125).
- Capital expenditure – the cost of computers, cars, machinery, etc. – or expenditure involving improvement as distinct from the repair of an asset. Instead, claim capital allowances where possible.
- Entertaining either UK or overseas customers.
- Your own earnings.
- Class 2 and Class 4 NICs (see page 132).
- Donations to political parties and charitable donations that do not directly benefit your business.

Example of business accounts and a tax computation

It has been assumed that John Wiltshire has been in business for several years, as there are special rules for new businesses.

John Wiltshire – Florists Profit and loss account for year ended 5 April 2011			
	£		£
Opening stock	750	Sales or takings	79,200
Purchases	22,000	Closing stock	2,500
Gross profit	58,950		
	£81,700		£81,700
Staff wages and NIC	6,842	Gross profit	58,950
Rent and rates	14,126	Rent receivable	750
Telephone	427	Profit on sale of	
Light and heat	623	motor car	398
Legal fees re new lease	100	Interest received (gross)	105
Insurance of shop	181		
Motor expenses	512		
Travelling/entertaining	107		
Postage and stationery	87		
General expenses	202		
Bank charges and interest	64		
Depreciation:			
Motor car	600		
Fixtures	376		
Repairs and renewals	789		
Wife's wages	980		
Own wages	20,000		
Own NIC	278		
	46,294		
Net profit	13,909		
	£60,203		£60,203

Although John Wiltshire will start with these accounts, various adjustments will have to be made to arrive at an adjusted profit for tax purposes. A tax computation based on the accounts will have to be prepared as shown on the next page:

John Wiltshire – Florists
Profit adjusted for income tax for year ended 5 April 2011

		£	£
Profit per accounts			13,909
Less: Income taxed separately:			
Rent received		750	
Interest received gross		105	
Profit on sale of motor car		398	
			1,253
			12,656
Add: Items not allowable for tax purposes:			
Own wages and NIC		20,278	
Repairs and renewals – new till		525	
Depreciation: Motor car		600	
Fixtures		376	
General expenses – donations		22	
Entertaining customers		66	
Motor expenses – 20 per cent private use		102	
Legal fees re new lease		100	
			22,069
			34,725
Less: Capital allowances		1,100	
Less: Private use of car	£ 220		
Balancing charge re motor car	144		
		364	
			736
Taxable profit			£ 33,989

John Wiltshire – Florists
Tax computation

John Wiltshire's tax liability is as follows for 2010–2011:

		£
Taxable profit (as above)		£ 33,989
Rent	£750	
Interest received gross	105	855
		34,844
Deduct: Personal allowance		6,475
Taxable income		£ 28,369
Total income tax payable		
£28,369 at 20 per cent		5,673
Class 4 NIC payable: £33,989 – £5,715 (lower limit)		
= £28,274 at 8 per cent		2,261
Class 2 NIC £2.40 × 52		125
Total tax and NIC		£8,059

Notes

1. If Mrs Wiltshire's wages are going to be her only income next year, she will lose part of her own personal allowance if they stay at their current low level. It would be more tax advantageous to increase her wages to utilise her full allowance and thus reduce the tax paid by John on his profits.

2. John will make payments on account of his tax and NIC liability on 31 January and 31 July 2011, paying (or receiving) any balance on 31 January 2012.

3. If John's taxable profit had exceeded £43,875 he would have paid an extra 1 per cent on the excess in NI contributions.

Pension contributions

Refer to page 163.

Capital allowances

You should set aside part of your profits to save for the replacement of those assets which either become worn out or obsolete. This provision would be shown as depreciation in your accounts.

As mentioned in the previous section, your depreciation provisions are ignored for tax purposes and instead you can claim capital allowances (see table overleaf) as a tax deduction.

There are three types of capital allowances – an annual investment allowance, a writing down allowance and a first year allowance. All eligible plant and machinery is grouped ('pooled' in HMRC language) according to their writing down percentages. The balance remaining in each pool, after deducting that years allowance is carried forward to the following year and it is this next balance to which the writing down allowance is applied. Assets that you use in part privately have to be grouped in separate pools.

Special apportionment rules apply when a business begins or ceases.

Remember that you can claim capital allowances on assets that you transfer to the business when you start up (such as furniture, car, etc.).

If you use a business asset for private purposes – for instance, a motor car for the weekends and holidays – you must reduce the allowances by the proportion representing your private use.

If one year's business profit was small enough to be covered by your tax allowances, or you had suffered a trading loss so that you pay no tax, then it may be more worthwhile for you not to claim the whole of the capital allowances; this would keep the written down value for tax purposes higher to give you larger writing down allowances to set against your future profits.

Buying plant and machinery

It is normally better to buy plant or equipment on the last day of one financial year rather than the first day of your next year – the reason being that you get the equivalent of a full year's capital allowance even though you have owned it for only a matter of hours and, although legally yours, have not necessarily paid for it. You need not actually pay the whole purchase price – you can buy on hire purchase.

Selling plant and machinery

You deduct the proceeds of any sale from the appropriate pool before calculating the writing down allowance. If the proceeds exceed the total value of the pool, after adding the additions for the year, the excess will be charged to tax as a 'balancing charge'. If the proceeds do not exceed the total value of the pool, after adding the additions for the year, the difference will be deducted from your profits (or added to your losses) for tax purposes. This is called a 'balancing allowance'.

If you expect to dispose of an asset within two years for less than the tax written down value, you can elect within two years of the year of acquisition to 'depool' the asset.

Capital allowances			
	2009–2010 per cent	2010–2011 per cent	2011–2012 per cent
Plant and machinery			
First year allowance	40	–	–
Annual investment allowance	100	100	100
– maximum on capital expenditure in a year	£50,000	£100,000	£100,000*
Annual writing down allowance on reducing balance – main pool	20	20	20**
– special pool	10	10	10***
Motor cars			
First year allowance for cars with CO_2 emissions not exceeding 110g/km	100	100	100
Annual writing down allowance on reducing balance on cars with 160g/km emissions or less	20	20	20
As above, but with emissions higher than 160g/km	10	10	10

*Reducing from April 2012 to *£25,000; **18 per cent; ***8 per cent.*

Notes
1. There are 100 per cent first-year allowances available on certain environmentally friendly equipment, the renovation of business premises and, from March 2011, for electric vans.
2. You van claim a 4 per cent writing down allownce on factories, warehouses, agricultural and hotel buildings and houses under assured tenancies schemes.
3. The list of assets that have special capital allowances is now fairly extensive; for a full list, log on to **www.hmrc.gov.uk**.

Short life assets

For any plant and machinery purchased after April 2011 that has a likely working life of no more than eight years (previously four years) then you can elect for it to be treated individually for capital allowance purposes and identified in a separate pool – you would adopt such an election if, for example, your annual investment allowances had been used up.

Small pools allowance

If the balance on the main, or special pool, is under £1,000 after adjusting for current years additions and disposals, then the whole balance can be written off against profits.

Research and development tax relief

This relief for small and medium-sized enterprises is increased to 200 per cent (previously 175 per cent) from 1 April 2011 and will increase further to 225 per cent from 1 April 2012.

Your tax assessments

For existing businesses

Profits are assessed to tax based on the accounts year ending during the tax year; for example, accounts made up for the year ended 30 June 2010 would be the basis for the 2010–2011 tax computation, those made up to 5 April 2010 would be for 2009–2010.

For new businesses

The date to which you prepare accounts is entirely up to you. Special rules of assessment apply for the first two tax years. For example, if your first accounts are for year ended 30 June 2010, your tax computations will be based as follows:

- Year one 2009–2010: On the profit earned between the 1 July 2009 starting date and 5 April 2010 (apportioned on a time basis).

- Year two 2010–2011: On the profit earned for the first 12 months of trading (that is year ended 30 June 2010.)

- Year three 2011–2012: On the accounts for the year ended 30 June 2011.

As you will see in the above example, part of the first year's profits are taxed twice in years one and two (1 July 2009 to 5 April 2010). This is referred to as the overlap profit and details should be kept of the overlapping period and profit, as you are able to claim overlap relief if your business ceases or, in certain circumstances, you change the date to which you draw up your accounts.

Your tax bills

You pay tax on your adjusted profit less capital allowances, personal allowances and deductions you will have claimed in your tax return.

Your total tax bill is normally payable in two equal instalments on 31 January and 31 July in each year, to which is added any Class 4 national insurance contributions (see page 132). Any tax that has been deducted from trading income (other than subcontractors in the construction industry) can be offset.

If you are in a partnership, the partnership profits will still need to be agreed in the firm's name and no partner can independently agree just his or her own share of the profits. However, the tax liability for each partner will be calculated separately, taking into account each partner's personal allowances and reliefs. Partners are no longer responsible for the other partners' tax liabilities.

Trading losses

If you make a loss, then enter the figures in your tax return, or write to your tax office advising them of the fact.

You can either, first offset the loss against other income and gains of the same tax year, then against previous years profits; (note that since November 2008 you have been able to carry back trading losses up to a maximum of £50,000 to relieve any taxable profits of the previous three years); or you can carry the loss forward to be relieved against future profits. This limit does not apply in the first four years of a new business, nor in the year that a business ceases.

You cannot claim all your tax reliefs and only a *part* of any loss; you must claim the whole of the loss first. Therefore before making a claim for loss relief, you should calculate whether you would lose a significant proportion of your personal allowances and deductions.

If, after deducting the loss as suggested above, you find that the remaining income is insufficient to cover your personal allowances, it may be better to carry forward the whole loss with a view to setting it off against future profits from the same trade.

National insurance contributions

Another liability you have while running your own business is national insurance contributions. Refer to Chapter 14 on page 132 for details.

Selling up or retiring?

Whether you sell the business, retire, or stop trading for any other reason, you could be faced with revised tax liabilities as profits are assessed differently in the closing years. Refer also to Chapter 15 for any capital gains tax exposure.

Post cessation receipts

If you receive monies after a business has been discontinued and tax assessments have been finalised, you must declare such income in the *Additional information* pages (see page 61) in your tax return. Any 'late' relevant expenditure can be offset against such receipts for tax purposes or shown separately (see page 64).

If your other income in the year of payment of post cessation expenses is not sufficient to utilise the relief in full, then a claim can be made for the excess to be treated as an allowable loss for capital gains purposes.

Employed or self-employed?

To establish whether you are employed or self-employed for tax purposes will depend on a number of factors. The tax office will consider whether you invest in your business, risk capital and provide substantial equipment and materials; also whether you work for a fixed number of hours at another's premises under the direction of a third party, or you are free to come and go as you please. The number of clients you have will also be taken into consideration.

Each case is judged on its merits and the tax office will give an opinion if asked. The website at **www.hmrc.gov.uk** will give you further information.

Managed personal service companies

The tax authorities continue to seek to treat people who provide their services via an intermediary such as a service company, and enter into working arrangements with clients which have the characteristics of employment, as an employee of that client for tax and NIC purposes.

The tax authorities are concerned at the loss of revenue by virtue of the fact that, for instance, the service company can invoice the client without deducting PAYE or national insurance contributions and the person can then take money out of the company in the form of, say, dividends rather than salary, thus avoiding NICs and gaining other tax advantages.

New definitions of managed and personal service companies (known as IR35 rules) were introduced and there are provisions to compel such companies to operate PAYE and Class 1 national insurance on all payments received by individuals in respect of services provided through such companies.

There is a specific section of the tax return dealing with service companies (see page 30).

Several test cases are still being explored through the courts.

Provisions also exist for HMRC to charge corporation tax on dividends and distributions paid to non-company shareholders by close companies.

For further information on this complicated topic, go to **www.hmrc.gov.uk/ir35**.

CHAPTER 14

National insurance

Unless you can get exemption on the grounds of low earnings, old age or incapacity, everyone has to pay national insurance on earnings from their employment, or on profits from being self-employed. It is compulsory and therefore a further tax on income.

National insurance contributions

By law, all employers have to deduct a national insurance contribution (NIC) from an employee's pay over a certain limit and pass it on to the tax office, together with the employer's contribution. National insurance contributions are levied on earnings over certain limits and are not allowed as a deduction for tax purposes.

'Earnings' for NIC purposes include pay, bonuses, fees, benefits, etc. and any non-business payments made by your employer on your behalf. There are lower scales of NI contributions for employees who have contracted out of the State pension scheme and who are members of an approved employer's scheme.

There are six types of national insurance contribution:

1. **Class 1.** Earnings-related contributions payable by most employees, including directors. Employers also have to pay a contribution.

2. **Class 1A.** Payable by the employer on most benefits paid to employees.

3. **Class 1B.** Payable by employers for PAYE settlement agreements.

4. **Class 2.** A flat rate payable by self-employed persons.

5. **Class 3.** If, for some reason, your contribution record under Classes 1 and 2 is inadequate for you to qualify for some NI benefits, you can pay voluntary contributions to make up your record.

6. **Class 4.** Earnings-related contributions payable by self-employed persons and assessed at the same time as income tax. These payments are in addition to Class 2 contributions.

You are exempt from paying Class 4 contributions for 2011–2012 if, on 6 April 2011, you are a man aged 65 (or a woman aged 60) or over or if you are under 16 or you are non-resident for tax purposes.

There are also exemptions if you are infirm.

A table giving all the rates is reproduced on pages 134–135.

The NI contributions office have a helpline for employees on 0191 225 3002 and for employers on 0845 7143143.

If you have more than one employer or both employment and self-employment income, then at the end of the year you can either defer or claim back any national insurance deductions made in excess of the annual maximum by writing to the NICO Refunds Group at Longbenton, Newcastle upon Tyne NE98 1ZZ.

NICs on company benefits

Where taxable benefits are given to employees (see page 72), then any amounts taxable on individuals and shown on their P11D forms are liable to employer's Class 1A national insurance contributions at 13.8 per cent for 2011–2012. This additional NIC liability is payable by the employer annually in arrears in July.

The tax office issue a free guide (CWG5) which shows those benefits that are liable and those that are exempt from this NI charge. Those that are liable are also identified on the P11D form.

Contracting out

There are lower scales of NI contributions for employees who have contracted out of the State earnings-related pension scheme and who are members of an approved employer's scheme.

Individuals may also contract out via an appropriate personal pension scheme and have a proportion of both their employer's and their own national insurance contributions, referred to as the contracted-out rebate, paid into their own personal pension plan.

Self-employed

All self-employed people are liable to pay flat rate Class 2 NICs either by a direct payment or direct debit through a bank, etc.

If your earnings from self-employment in 2011–2012 are going to be less than £5,315 you may apply at the local tax office to be exempted on the grounds of small earnings.

Inform the tax office if Class 2 contributions are not due for any period (for example, if you are incapacitated). Alternatively, as the contributions are now set at the low rate of £2.50 per week, you may prefer to continue to pay Class 2 and thereby maintain your record of contributions.

In addition, you may be liable to pay a Class 4 contribution based on your profits chargeable to tax after deducting any capital allowances.

If, in addition to running your own business, you also have earnings from an employment on which you pay PAYE tax, then you may be liable to pay additional Class 1 national insurance contributions. However, there is an upper limit on your total liability – ask your tax office for an explanatory booklet or telephone the helpline on 0845 915 4655. New businesses can contact 0845 915 4515.

In these circumstances you may be eligible to apply for a deferral of Class 4 NI contributions rather than wait to claim a refund at the end of the year. However, deferment will only apply to the main NI rate and you will still be liable at the 2 per cent rate on all profits over the upper limit.

An application for deferral or exemption has to be done annually and there are strict time limits.

Pension forecast

See page 168 as to how to get a state pension forecast.

Married women

If you are paying reduced national insurance rates, it may be beneficial for you to cancel this election if you are below the minimum earning level – that way you will not have to pay national insurance but could still build up entitlement to benefits.

In calculating a wife's pension, the number of years of contributions is relevant – women need 30 qualifying years if you reach State pension age before 6 April 2010 (before that date qualifying years were 39), but note that:

- You can make backdated voluntary contributions (Class 3). Telephone 0845 915 5996 to check if you have a shortfall and whether it is beneficial to top up your contributions.

- Home responsibilities protection (HRP) (for example, being at home looking after children or getting income support because you are caring for a disabled person) does not give you a credit on your pension record, but reduces the number of qualifying years.

HRP credit is probably not in any pension forecast that you may get from the pension service as it is not given automatically, so do challenge the figures if you have been involved in HRP.

More than one NI number?

The number of employees that seem to have more than one national insurance number seems to be increasing and it is obviously a worry in that you might miss out on having an accurate payment record and this may affect your benefit entitlement – particularly to the State pension. If you are in this position, write to the Account Investigation Section, Banburgh House, Room BP1002, Benton Park View, Longbenton, Newcastle upon Tyne NE98 1ZZ.

National insurance contributions		
	2010–2011	2011–2012
Employee and employer rates and thresholds in £ per week unless stated		
Lower earnings limit (LEL) for Class 1 NICs	£97.00	£102.00
Upper earnings limit (UEL) for employee's (primary) Class 1 NICs	£844.00	£817.00
Upper accrual point (UAP)	£770.00	£770.00
Primary threshold	£110.00	£139.00
Secondary threshold	£110.00	£136.00
Employee's (primary) Class 1 contribution rates		
2010–2011 weekly earnings from £110.01 to £844.00 earnings limit	11%	N/A
2010–2011 weekly earnings above £844.00	1%	N/A
2011–2012 weekly earnings from £139.01 to £817.00	N/A	12%
2011–2012 weekly earnings above £817.00	N/A	2%
Employee's contracted out rebate		
For both salary-related (COSR) and money purchase (COMP) schemes between LEL and UAP	1.6%	1.6%
Married women's reduced rate for (primary) Class 1 contribution rates*		
2010–2011 weekly earnings from £110.01 to £844.00 earnings limit	4.85%	N/A
2010–2011 weekly earnings above £844.00	1%	N/A
2011–2012 weekly earnings from £139.01 to £817.00	N/A	5.85%
2011–2012 weekly earnings above £817.00	N/A	2%
Employer's (secondary) Class 1 contribution rates		
2010–2011 weekly earnings above £110.00	12.8%	N/A
2011–2012 weekly earnings above £136.00	N/A	13.8%
Employer's contracted-out rebate		
Employer's contracted-out rebate, salary related schemes (COSR) beween LEL and UAP	3.7%	3.7%
Employer's contracted-out rebate, money purchase schemes (COMP) between LEL and UAP	1.4%	1.4%

*The reduced rate applies to women married before 6 April 1977 who have elected to pay a reduced rate of Class 1 contributions.

National insurance contributions

Self-employed and others – rates and thresholds
(£ per week unless stated)

	2010–2011	2011–2012
Class 2 National insurance contributions*		
Self-employed, Class 2 NICs	£2.40	£2.50
Small earnings annual exemption level, Class 2 NICs	£5,075	£5,315
Volunteer development workers, Class 2 NICs	£4.85	£5.10
Share fishermen, Class 2 NICs	£3.05	£3.15
Class 3 National insurance contributions		
Voluntary contributions	£12.05	£12.60
Class 4 National insurance contributions		
2010–2011 annual profits below lower profits limit of £5,715	Nil	N/A
2010–2011 annual profits above lower profits limit of £5,715 but below upper profits limit of £43,875	8%	N/A
2010–2011 annual profits above upper profits limit of £43,875	1%	N/A
2011–2012 annual profits below lower profits limit of £7,225	N/A	Nil
2011–2012 annual profits above lower profits limit of £7,225 but below upper profits limit of £42,475	N/A	9%
2011–2012 annual profits above upper profits limit of £42,475	N/A	2%

*Class 2 NICs are paid by all self-employed persons. Those with profits less than, or expected to be less than, the level of the small earnings exception may apply for exemption from paying Class 2 contributions.

CHAPTER 15

Capital gains tax

The earlier chapters in this book dealt with tax that may be payable on *income* (that is, your earnings, pensions, investment income, etc.).

You may also be liable to pay tax on *gains* from assets and possessions, for example, land and buildings, shares, antiques, paintings or a business, when such assets change hands. The taxation of capital gains has always been complicated, although it was significantly simplified in the 2008 budget. Only a concise summary is given here in order to provide background knowledge. If in doubt, seek professional advice.

This chapter deals specifically with disposals by individuals. There are special rules for business assets (but see page 139) and interests in trusts, which are outside the scope of this book.

What is a capital gain?

A capital gain is any profit arising when you sell, transfer, give, receive compensation for, or otherwise dispose of any of your assets or possessions. There is no capital gains tax payable on death but instead your estate may be liable to pay inheritance tax (see Chapter 16 on page 142).

Is there such a thing as a capital loss?

Yes; obviously it is the reverse of a capital gain, and any capital losses are deducted from any capital gains that you make in the same year. If your capital losses exceed your capital gains, then you cannot claim tax back, but you can carry forward the losses against future gains.

Assets that are exempted from capital gains

The most important asset for most people will be your own house. If it is owned and occupied by you and is your main residence, this is *free of capital gains tax* – but see pages 81 and 140 if it is part-let or used for business. Thus a husband and wife, and same-sex couples who have entered into a statutory civil registration since 5 December 2005, can have only one main residence between them; a couple who cohabit can have one residence each and are thus technically in a more favourable position tax wise.

Perhaps the second most important exemption is transfers of assets between married couples and civil partners. These are treated as taking place for no capital profit or loss; this does not apply if the parties are separated or divorced.

Other exempted assets are:

- Chattels – such as jewellery, pictures and furniture – where the proceeds are £6,000 or less; if the proceeds exceed £6,000, the gain is the lower of the proceeds less cost, or proceeds less £6,000 multiplied by 5/3 (this limit has remained at this level since 1970!).
- Child trust funds.
- Compensation for personal or professional injury.
- Decorations for gallantry, unless purchased.
- Foreign currency for personal use.
- Gambling, pools and lottery winnings and prizes.
- Gifts to amateur sports clubs open to the whole community.
- Gifts of outstanding public interest given to the nation.
- Gifts to charities.
- Government stocks and public corporation stocks.
- A house owned and occupied by you which is your main residence. If part let, see page 140, and for claims for use of your home as your office see page 81.
- Individual savings accounts (ISAs).
- Interests in certain settled property.
- Land and buildings given to the National Trust.
- Life policies and deferred annuities (unless sold on by original owner).
- Motor cars (private).
- National Savings certificates; premium bonds.
- Pension plans (registered).
- Qualifying corporate bonds.
- Save as You Earn schemes.
- Shares subscribed for under the enterprise investment scheme (EIS).
- Shares subscribed for in approved quoted venture capital trusts.
- Wasting assets with a likely life of 50 years or less.

Annual exemption

You are allowed to make capital gains of £10,600 (£10,100 in 2010–2011) in each year (after deducting capital losses) before you are liable to pay capital gains tax. Most trusts are exempt on the first £5,300 (£5,050 in 2010–2011).

How to avoid capital gains tax

The main step to take is to ensure that you are making full use of the 'free of tax' list above. For example, do consider putting some of your savings into ISAs, pension schemes, National Savings, Government stocks and various enterprise schemes.

If you do hold shares and other assets that can be readily sold, manage them in such a way that you take advantage of the annual exemption amounts. Married couples and civil partners each get the annual exemption in their own right, but losses cannot be offset between husband and wife, nor between partners.

Transfers of assets made between married couples and civil partners are treated as taking place for no capital gain or loss if they are living together. This does not apply if the parties are separated or divorced.

Rates of tax

Prior to 6 April 2008, an individual paid capital gains tax on gains above the annual exemption limit at income tax rates as if the gains were savings added to total income. You may therefore have been liable to capital gains tax at the starting rate (10 per cent), savings rate (20 per cent) or higher rate (40 per cent) depending on your other income.

There was also an indexation allowance and, subsequently, tapering relief to compensate for inflation.

If you need details of capital gains tax calculations prior to April 2008 then you need to refer to the 2008–2009 edition of this book.

From 6 April 2008, all the above rates were replaced by a flat rate of 18 per cent on all personal capital gains until 23 June 2010, since when if your gains plus your other total taxable income take you into the higher-rate tax threshhold, then your capital gains tax rate will be 28 per cent.

How to calculate a capital gain or loss

Excluding those assets that are free of capital gains tax, you need to note the original cost of all assets sold (any assets held as at 31 March 1982 are valued as at that date, not at their original cost). The cost price is the purchase price (probate or market value if not purchased) plus acquisition expenses.

This cost price is then deducted from the sales proceeds, (from which you can deduct any sales costs and any sums spent on improving the asset as distinct from just maintaining it), and the resultant figure is your capital gain (or loss) for the year. Deduct from this figure your annual exemption (above).

If your gain is below the annual exemption figure then there is no tax to pay.

If the gain is higher than the annual exemption figure then you can offset any losses brought forward from the previous year, and if a gain still results then you pay tax at 28 or 18 per cent (see previous page).

If you have made a net capital loss in the year you can carry this forward to the next year to, hopefully, offset against future capital gains. The above applies to personal assets – for business assets see below.

Paying capital gains tax

Capital gains tax is payable, with any balance of income tax due, on the 31 January following each year. If you sell an asset on which you have a capital gain on the 6 April rather than on 5 April you will have an extra year before having to pay the capital gains tax.

Capital gains tax can be deferred by subscribing for new shares through the enterprise investment scheme (EIS) or new shares in approved quoted venture capital trusts (VCT); in such cases the capital gains tax deferral is in addition to the 20 per cent income tax relief (see page 162).

Business assets

The capital gains legislation has always been very complicated and there has always been special categories of business that have had their own exemptions, rules and regulations. It is important to seek professional advice.

There is an entrepreneur's relief whereby capital gains from selling a business is only levied at 10 per cent; the maximum eligible amount was £5m up to 5 April 2011, increasing to £10m from that date, although this is now defined as a lifetime limit.

Business roll-over relief

This relief allows you to defer the capital gains tax bill when you sell or dispose of assets in your business, providing you replace them within three years after the sale (or the 12 months prior to the sale).

The whole of the sale proceeds must be so re-invested to defer the entire gain.

You can make a claim for roll-over relief within five years from 31 January following the end of the relevant tax year.

What to enter in your 2011 tax return

Refer to page 54 where the *Capital gains* supplementary pages are reproduced.

Remembering that the 2011 tax return will apply to capital gains for the year ending 5 April 2011, if your total proceeds of sale do not exceed £40,400 and/or your chargeable gains do not exceed £10,100, there is no need to make any entry at all in this part of your tax return unless you are claiming allowable losses or wish to make some other claim or election. However, it is wise to keep all your schedules and working notes.

As already mentioned, the capital gains tax legislation is very complicated – only a brief outline has been given here. There are, for example, complex rules for valuing assets held before the introduction of this tax in 1965; there are 'pooling' provisions for identical shares acquired on different dates; there are special rules for business assets and connected persons.

Inherited assets (chargeable assets acquired)

Contrary to many people's belief, you do not generally have to pay capital gains tax on receiving cash or assets left to you under a will or settlement. Assets only become liable (subject to the normal exemption rules) when you dispose of them. The probate value will be used as the base cost of these assets.

Selling or letting your house

Any profit you make on selling the property you own and live in is free from capital gains tax. Where you own two houses at the same time as a result of not being able to sell the first, no capital gains will arise on either house provided you sell the first house within three years. See page 155 for divorced persons.

Get professional advice if you plan to sell off part of your garden – there are complicated capital gains tax rules.

Many people worry that if they let part of their home, then they will have to pay capital gains tax on part of the profits they make when it is sold. In fact, you can claim letting relief to reduce any capital gains liability.

You do this by working out what proportion the let part of the property bears to the total and apply this to any capital profit. Against that profit you can claim capital gains tax letting relief of the lower of £40,000 or the apportioned gain before any capital gains tax liability is assessed.

The last three years of ownership of your home always counts as a period of residence, so if you move out and let the property during that time it will not affect your exemption.

Working from home

If you use part of your house exclusively for business then, when you sell the house, you may be liable to capital gains tax on that proportion that was used for business purposes although roll-over relief could apply (see page 139). This is unlikely to apply if you are an employee working from home occasionally unless a material part of the house is in fact used exclusively for business.

Seek professional advice

If your financial affairs are not too complicated, capital gains tax can be fairly straightforward. However, only a brief outline of the tax has been covered in this book, so do seek professional advice if you are in any way unclear about the taxable effects of selling or gifting assets.

For more background information the tax office issue a free leaflet, CGT/FS1, available from any tax office.

CHAPTER 16

Inheritance tax

Most of the chapters in this book have dealt with tax payable on your income. Chapter 15 dealt with tax payable on capital items (capital gains tax) when such assets change hands during your lifetime.

Having paid all such liabilities, you are *still* not free of the tax inspector, for inheritance tax may have to be considered. Inheritance tax may be payable not only on the value of your estate on death, but also on lifetime gifts.

Most taxes have complex rules and provisions, mainly to avoid fraud, and this tax is certainly no exception. In this book it is only possible to deal broadly with the main provisions and exemptions. You should consult an accountant or solicitor if you need specific planning advice, or if you have to deal with someone else's estate.

It used to be assumed that this tax was only paid by those who were fairly rich, but the exemption limit for inheritance tax is only £325,000. With the appreciation in value of private house prices in particular over the last ten years, plus any savings, investments and other assets you may have, and maybe proceeds from life assurance and pension fund lump sums, then more and more people are beginning to realise that this tax is in fact applicable to them, and when they die, their estate will have to pay a large tax bill unless they do something about it now and consider some inheritance planning measures.

Exemption limits and rates of tax

On deaths arising after 5 April 2009, an estate is liable to pay inheritance tax at a flat rate of 40 per cent on the value of the net assets, including any home you own, in excess of £325,000. From April 2012 you will be able to claim a reduction in the rate of tax if part of your estate is left to charity (see page 10).

Any unused proportion on the first death of a married couple, or civil partner can be added to a remaining partner's exemption limit where that second death was on or after 8 October 2007.

In other words, if, say on the death of the first partner, 50 per cent of the exemption amount was not used, then that percentage could be added to the exemption amount available to the remaining partner.

If you have married more than once, then you cannot utilise more than two tax-free exemption bands.

The estate of someone who dies on active service is exempt from inheritance tax.

What is the value of your estate for inheritance purposes?

You need to identify six sets of figures as follows:

- List all your assets at their current value, including ISAs which lose their tax-free benefits when you die;
- Deduct any outstanding liabilities (mortgages, loans etc.) and any tax free legacies stated in your will (see below);
- Add any likely life assurance receipt (although you can avoid this – see page 148) and any unused pension fund passing to your family;
- Add any potentially exempt gifts you have made in the previous seven years after allowing for any tax free gifts (see page 145);
- Add any gifts with reservation (see page 145) or pre-owned asset.

The total of this calculation is now the net value of your estate for inheritance tax purposes.

Note that an additional tax charge may be payable during your lifetime on certain chargeable lifetime transfers and pre-owned assets (see page 144).

Remember that all assets passing between married couples and civil partners either by bequest under a will or under the rules governing the estate of anyone dying intestate (that is someone who has not made a will) are free of inheritance tax regardless of the total value.

HMRC have a leaflet (IHT 15) *Inheritance tax; how to calculate the liability*, available free from tax offices or their website.

The following paragraphs give more detail about the various gifts and transfers that might arise when considering this incredibly complicated tax.

Tax-free legacies on death

The following legacies are allowed as a deduction from your estate for inheritance tax purposes:

- Legacies made for the benefit of the nation or for the public benefit, including funds to maintain historic property.
- Legacies made between husband and wife and civil partners, provided both are domiciled in the UK.
- Legacies to a charity.

- Legacies to political parties.
- Legacies of certain heritage property and woodlands.

Lifetime gifts

Gifts fall into three categories as far as the inheritance tax rules are concerned: some gifts are specifically tax free and can be ignored; other gifts are exempt, provided they were not made within seven years of death; and the third category covers chargeable lifetime transfers and gifts with reservation.

Tax-free gifts

The following are gifts which are exempt:

- All gifts between a husband and wife and between civil partners, if both are domiciled in the UK (if not, the limit is £55,000).
- Gifts up to a total of £3,000 in any one year plus any unused amount of the previous year's exemption. (You can carry over unused relief for a maximum of one year.)
- In addition to the £3,000 referred to above, individual gifts not exceeding £250 each to different persons in any one tax year (to an unlimited number of people as long as they don't form part of a larger gift).
- Additional gifts if a person makes them as part of normal habitual expenditure made out of income.
- Gifts arranged beforehand in consideration of marriage or civil partnership as follows:

	Maximum gift limit £
Parents of either	5,000 each
Grandparents or more remote relatives of either	2,500
Any other person	1,000

(The gifts must be made before the actual wedding day.)

- All gifts to qualifying political parties, or UK-established charities.
- Lump sums received from a pension scheme on death or retirement if used to purchase a pension for yourself or dependants.
- Gifts for the benefit of the nation or the general public (for example, universities, the National Trust).
- Maintenance payments to ex-husbands, ex-wives or ex-civil partners.
- Reasonable gifts to support a dependant relative.

- Gifts for the education and maintenance of your children, if under 18 years of age.
- Gifts of decorations for valour, etc., if they have never been sold.

All other gifts within seven years of death

These are known as potentially exempt transfers (PETs) and are tax free once you have lived for seven years from making the gift. If you die before the end of the seven-year period, the value of the gift is added to your estate for inheritance tax purposes, although there is a reduction in the *tax payable* on the gift on a tapering scale as follows:

Years between gift and death	0–3	3–4	4–5	5–6	6–7
Percentage of inheritance tax payable	100	80	60	40	20

It is important to note that potentially exempt transfers are deducted from the nil rate exemption threshold *before* applying the balance of the exemption to the rest of the estate.

Gifts with reservation

These are gifts you have made but from which you continue to benefit, for example, gifting your house but continuing to live in it yourself without paying a market rent.

Chargeable lifetime transfers and pre-owned assets

Prior to April 2006, it was quite common for individuals to avoid (or reduce) any future inheritance tax liability by setting up various forms of trust. However, since that date legislation has been enacted that substantially reduces these benefits, or creates another tax charge.

Similarly some individuals made arrangements to reduce their inheritance tax liability by gifting or selling an asset at below its full market value by way of a trust but who continued to benefit from that asset.

Since 6 April 2005 any such benefit can attract a 'pre-owned asset' tax charge.

The taxable benefit is calculated on the market rent value in the case of land or property and in the case of other assets the benefit is considered to be 4.75 per cent per year of its market value. No tax charge arises where the benefit is less than £5,000 per year and it does not apply to assets you ceased to own prior to 18 March 1986.

A gift to most trusts, except mainly those set up for the benefit of disabled people and bereaved children, and employee benefit trusts, is now liable to a tax charge of some sort depending on the type of trust. The legislation is complicated and you almost certainly need to seek professional advice, for there are a number of exclusions and transitional reliefs. Details of any benefit arising has to be declared in your main tax return.

There is a website for further information on **www.hmrc.gov.uk/poa** – also ask your tax office for leaflets IHT 500 and IHT 501 by telephoning 0845 234 1000.

Who pays the inheritance tax bill?

The executors of an estate have to send an account to HMRC of all the taxable assets left at the date of death – see the HMRC website or telephone helpline 0845 302 0900, although it is probably best for a solicitor to handle these matters to ensure that you do everything possible to limit any inheritance liability.

It is the responsibility of the executors of a will to pay any taxes due within six months from the date of death before distributing the assets to the beneficiaries.

In the case of gifts made within the seven-year rule, executors could ask the person receiving the gift to pay the tax relating to the value of that gift, unless there is a clause in the will specifically authorising the estate to be responsible for paying any tax due, or the estate has insufficient funds to pay any tax liability.

Quick-succession relief

If a second death in a family occurs within five years of the first death the second tax bill is reduced by the ratio that the value of the estate on the first death bears to the value at the second death, to which needs to be added any inheritance tax paid on that first death. For example, assume the value of the estate at the first death was £700,000, on which inheritance tax was paid, and the estate value at the second death was £800,000, then the inheritance tax bill on the estate of the second death would be reduced by the ratio 5:4.

Under quick-succession relief, if there was more than one year between the deaths, the calculation is reduced by 20 per cent for each full year.

Small businesses and agricultural concerns

Over the past few years, most budgets have extended reliefs to reduce the impact of inheritance tax on the transfer of interests in small businesses and agricultural concerns. There are now substantial inheritance tax concessions – often reducing the liability to zero – if you own such a business concern.

The rules, regulations and conditions, on the type of business and period of ownership prior to death, are numerous and complex. It is important to consult professional advisers when considering such matters.

Unmarried partners

Married couples and same-sex couples who are registered as civil partners are treated equally for all tax legislation. However, unmarried couples who live together do not get the same rights – they are treated as single persons for all tax legislation (but not for all social security legislation) so it is particularly important that each couple gives serious thought to the question of making a will and what happens to the home and property when one partner dies.

Ways to reduce inheritance tax exposure

Most tax schemes to reduce inheritance tax are inevitably aimed at married couples or those who have entered into civil partnerships.

The following ideas should be considered and discussed with your solicitor or an independent financial adviser who specialises in inheritance tax. Such professionals should ideally be members of the Society of Trust and Estate Practitioners (STEP). The society can be contacted for a list of members in your area on 020 7340 0500 or their website **www.step.org**.

- Make a will in order to make it clear to whom you wish your assets to pass on your death and to specify any personal wishes, gifts to family, friends, charities, etc., otherwise you will die intestate and cause unnecessary stress and problems for your family and dependants (see below).

- Consider holding savings, investments and other assets in joint names in order to spread the ownership and reduce individual estate valuations.

- Prior to October 2007, it had been thought prudent for married couples or civil partners to hold the deeds of their main residence as tenants in common, not as joint tenants, so that each partner's share (and it did not have to be in equal parts) was independent of the other and could be sold or given away as that party wished so that when one partner died only 50 per cent (or the agreed share) would be valued in their estate. Now that it is possible to transfer any unused inheritance tax exemption limit from a first death, this is not so significant but should still be considered.

- Giving assets away in your lifetime obviously has the likelihood of reducing any inheritance tax liability, but bear in mind there may be capital gains to consider.

- Life assurance should be considered, particularly for young to middle-aged partners, but do ensure the policy is written in trust otherwise any lump sum paid out on death will be added to your estate, thus increasing the probability of a higher inheritance tax liability.

- Certain investments, if held for a certain length of time, are exempt from inheritance tax. These include investments in woodlands, agricultural property or shares quoted on the alternative investment market (AIM) and enterprise investment schemes.

- As a last resort, if you are left property under a will, and you either do not want it or you wish to pass it on to someone else (perhaps to avoid future tax liabilities), then you can effect a deed of variation within two years of the date of death. Such a deed can also be used if someone dies without making a will.

- Always bear in mind that a settlor cannot also be a beneficiary – and you must relinquish all title and control over an asset if it is to escape the clutches of the inheritance tax net.

Wills

You should always make a will regardless of how much you own. This will prevent your dependants being unduly troubled and will mean that your wishes will be carried out legally and properly. Although there are do-it-yourself will packages available, it does not cost a lot to go through a solicitor, and you will then have expert, experienced advice on which to draw.

If you don't leave a valid will, you will be regarded as having died intestate and your assets will be distributed under strict legal rules, which may not be what you intended.

Many people make reference to specific charities in their will, stating to whom they would like to make legacies. The only problem with this is that if you wish to change the charities you have selected, you have to make a new will. You can get over this by leaving the legacies to the Charities Aid Foundation, giving them a list of the charities you wish to benefit. You can then change this list at any time, thus saving you the legal costs of changing your will.

The various law societies have lists of solicitors who specialise in wills and probate. In England and Wales the helpline is 020 7242 1222, in Scotland 0131 226 7411 and in Northern Ireland 028 9023 1614.

Pension schemes

If you have a pension scheme and you are approaching 75 and you have not yet organised an annuity, check with your pension adviser or solicitor to ensure the fund is not going to be liable to inheritance tax, (see page 167).

CHAPTER 17

Family tax matters

Whether you are starting your first job, getting married, saving money, working on your own or retiring, you cannot escape the tax inspector.

Many people experience great difficulty in commucating with their tax office for one reason or another, particularly in claiming tax repayments. The secret behind dealing with any tax matter is to comply with the system. The whole of our tax system revolves around filling in forms at the right time (see Chapter 3 on page 16).

Either telephone your tax office, or call in or write and ask for the correct form, depending upon your circumstances. Fill it in and send it to your tax office in order to start the ball rolling. Always state your tax reference number. These days many of the forms are also available on the website, www.hmrc.gov.uk, so you can download them from there.

If you are taxed under PAYE, write to the tax office that deals with your employer's PAYE. If you are self-employed you will deal with the inspector who covers your business address.

Here are some practical steps to bear in mind.

Starting work
PAYE
You will need a tax code number (see page 100).

Your employer will fill in a form P45 and give this to you. You then select which of the statements A, B or C applies to you, and complete the rest of the form.

If, however, you decide to work for yourself, or in partnership with someone else, you will eventually have to fill in a tax return on which you will claim your allowances and declare your income. Thus the PAYE system will not apply to you and all you need to do is to tell your tax office when your business commences (see page 119).

National insurance contributions
National insurance contributions are levied at varying rates depending on how much you earn, whether you are contracted out and whether you are an employee or self-employed. See Chapter 14 on page 131 for further details.

Changes in allowances and deductions

Most tax allowances and tax credits are not given to you automatically – they have to be claimed and the claim must be supported by the right information.

The more common instances of changes in allowances and credits are covered in this chapter.

Married couples and same-sex couples

Same-sex partners who registered their relationship in a civil partnership on or after 5 December 2005 are entitled to the same income tax, inheritance tax and pension and tax credits as married couples.

What should couples do to benefit fully from the tax system?

1. **Personal allowances.** Both partners get a personal allowance in their own right; it will be wasted if neither work and have no income at all – it cannot be transferred from one to the other. To avoid one partner losing the personal allowance, consider transferring investments or savings so that the income can be offset against the other partner's personal allowance.

2. **Married couple's allowance.** If one partner was born before 6 April 1935, then you can claim married couple's allowance. Refer to page 94 to see if it is beneficial to transfer this allowance.

3. **Higher rate tax.** If a husband or wife or partner is paying tax at higher rates than the basic rate, then transferring some income-producing assets between them would be beneficial if one partner is on the basic rate tax band or is not using all of their personal allowance. Sometimes a partner may be reluctant to transfer cash or assets in case they may be 'spent'. One solution is to transfer certain assets into joint ownership as 'tenants in common'. Whilst the original owner could retain, say, a 95 per cent share, the tax office would treat the income as being split 50:50 if no declaration of actual ownership is made. In some cases it may be beneficial to make a declaration of ownership, in which case ask the tax office for form 17 before the start of a tax year (you cannot backdate such a request).

4. **Age-related allowances.** Partners aged 65 and over should similarly check that their tax affairs are organised as above because both the higher personal allowance, which each of them gets in their own right, and the married couple's allowance, if applicable, are reduced if their incomes exceed certain limits (see page 113).

5. **Covenants and gift aid.** Ensure that tax relief on covenants and gift aid is not lost (see page 91).

6. **Capital gains.** If at all practicable, ensure that your investments are allocated between you or held in joint names so that you can each take full benefit of the capital gains exemption limit when investments are sold.

7. **Stakeholder pensions.** Each partner can pay up to £3,600 (including tax relief) a year into a stakeholder pension fund even if they have no earnings. Consider setting up pension funds for a non-working husband or wife or civil partner and/or children. Pensions generally are dealt with in more detail on page 163.

Raising a family

As soon as your baby is born, ask at your local benefits agency office for a child benefit claim form. Complete this and return it to them with the birth certificate.

Child benefit is normally payable to the mother and paid direct into her bank account each month (see page 185). The benefit is tax free.

Apply also for the child tax credit by telephoning 0845 300 3900 (see page 95).

Child trust funds

These were discontinued in respect of all babies born after 31 December 2010. Prior to that you were entitled to receive a voucher from the Government for £250 when you had a baby, and you could claim double this amount if you were entitled to the full child tax credit (see page 95); a further £250 (or £500) was paid when the child reached the age of seven but this ceased on 31 July 2010. You had to pay these vouchers into a bank or building society trust fund. Interest earned is free of income tax and capital gains tax.

Existing accounts can continue to be managed until the child's eighteenth birthday – no withdrawals are allowed prior to this.

Once the child reaches the age of 18 then he or she can use the money for any purpose whatsoever.

Additional funds can be invested in the trust account by parents or indeed anyone else (they do not have to be related to the child) up to an extra £1,200 a year, with a minimum contribution of £10. A fact sheet is available on the internet on **www.childtrustfund.gov.uk** or call the trust helpline on 0845 302 1470.

Childcare facilities

Employees can benefit from the use of childcare facilities provided by and paid for directly by their employer without incurring a tax or national insurance charge on that benefit.

To qualify for the exemption:

• The child must be under 18.

• The premises must not be domestic premises.

• The premises must be provided by the employer (or a group of employers or a local authority) with each employer(s) being responsible for finance and management.

Childcare voucher scheme

Employers can set aside up to £55 per week out of an employee's salary as a contribution towards the cost of registered childcare, including nurseries, nannies, crèches and after-school clubs, for under 16 year olds – in other words this is a specific salary sacrifice by the employee and it is free of income tax and national insurance. Each parent's employer can be involved in such a scheme, effectively giving a total of £110 per week as a maximum. Check that this benefit will not affect your tax credits for childcare costs.

Note that it was announced in the budget that those joining such a scheme after 6 April 2011 and who are liable for tax at either the 40 per cent or 50 per cent tax rates will have their relief restricted to £28 and £22 per week respectively. Refer to **www.hmrc.gov.uk/child care**.

This scheme is not available for the self-employed.

There is a useful website reference address you can visit on **www. daycaretrust.org.uk**.

Children's income

Each child is an individual taxpayer entitled to his or her own personal allowance. Parents are not taxable on a child's casual earnings nor on income arising on gifts from relatives. However, if you give cash or property to your children other than through the child trust fund scheme, the income will be treated as yours for income tax purposes if it exceeds £100 gross in the year.

In spite of the above, even if parents did give each of their children say £1,400 (outside the child trust fund), then at say 4 per cent this would still be under the 'taxable limit' and the interest would be tax free.

The only way in which parents could transfer larger sums to their children without continuing to pay tax on the income from those assets was by setting up an irrecoverable trust, which could accumulate income until the child was 18. However, if income was paid direct to the child before then, it was taxed as the income of the parent. You should consult a professional adviser regarding the current taxation legislation of trusts as it is a complicated subject and will vary according to a person's circumstances.

A child can receive, or benefit from, income provided by a relative, either by the gift of investments or by setting up a trust that pays out income for the child's education and maintenance. In these cases you should ask your tax office for form 232 on which to declare your child's income and, if the income has had tax deducted before receipt, for example trust income, interest, etc., claim a tax repayment in respect of the child's personal allowance.

Students

Earnings from holiday jobs will often have PAYE tax deducted. Ask your employer for form P38(S) which, when completed and returned, will enable payment to be made without tax deductions if the student does not earn above the personal allowance of £7,475 for 2011–2012 (£6,475 for 2010–2011).

Student loan repayments to a new borrower are collected under the PAYE system once employment commences, and the employer has to deduct repayments depending on the income level. These 'income contingent student loans', as they are called, have to be acknowledged in your tax return (see page 24).

If you change jobs frequently, your loan account could be incorrect, so it is important to check your annual statement regularly. You can also ring the helpline 0870 240 6298.

One-parent families

In addition to the personal allowance, you should consider claiming the various tax credits as detailed in Chapter 9 on page 95.

Divorce or separation

Inform the tax office of your changed circumstances. Obviously both parties keep their personal tax allowances and if you have been claiming married couple's allowance, then this will continue until the end of the tax year in which separation took place.

Any claim for child tax credit may have to be reassessed depending on which partner looks after the children – or, indeed, apportioned if a child is to spend some time living with each partner (see page 95). In the case of a woman who is paying national insurance contributions at the reduced rate, then you should reconsider your position to see if you need to pay full-rate contributions to protect your benefits. (Ask for leaflet CA10, National Insurance contributions for divorced women, available from your tax office.)

See page 90 regarding maintenance payments and page 168 for pension rights.

As regards the family home, if one partner sells, or gives it to the other within three years of the separation, then there will be no capital gains tax payable; and still no tax will be payable if, after that period, one of the partners still resides there and the other partner has not claimed any other property as a main home.

Death of a wife or husband or civil partner

On death, any married couple's allowance or blind person's allowance still unused is transferred to the surviving partner for the remainder of that tax year; similarly any unused inheritance tax exemption will be transferred to a remaining partner.

A tax-free bereavement payment can also be claimed from the Department for Work and Pensions (DWP) by either a widow, a widower or surviving civil partner, subject to certain conditions.

See Chapter 16 on page 142 regarding any inheritance tax liabilities.

Additionally, bereavement allowance and widowed parent's allowance might be available from the DWP, depending on your national insurance status and contributions.

Ceasing employment

Permanently

Send parts 2 and 3 of form P45, which your employer will have given you, to your tax office; the address is shown on the form. Also write a letter confirming that you have either retired, ceased working or have become self-employed, and claim any tax repayment.

Temporarily

When you change employment or are made redundant and there is a gap between one job and the next, you will need to hand in form P45 when you sign on to claim benefits. The Jobcentre Plus will advise you on the proportion of your jobseeker's allowance that is taxable and will deal with any tax refund due at the end of the tax year. Alternatively, if you are not entitled to benefits, send in your P45 to your tax office telling them you are temporarily unemployed. This may result in a tax refund.

If you do not start a new job by the following 5 April, check your total income and tax, as shown in Chapter 11 (page 103), to see if there is a repayment or underpayment of tax due, and if you have been claiming jobseeker's allowance or income support and you return to work then complete form ES40 and the Jobcentre will send you a P45 form for you to take to your new employer.

Making a will

It is important to make a will. See page 148 for more details.

Are you claiming your tax refund?

There are broadly two main categories of people who should consider claiming tax refunds:

Savers with building society and bank accounts

Interest paid by building societies and banks will have had tax deducted from it at the savings rate (20 per cent) before it is paid to you.

If your total income is less than your personal allowance – as will often be the case for children, husbands or wives or civil partners who are not earning or are on low incomes – then you should claim that tax back.

Ask your bank or building society for form R85, fill it in and return it to them. Once they have this form, they can pay you interest in future without first deducting tax.

Pensioners

The above comments also apply to pensioners but, in addition, many pensioners whose income is less than their age-related allowance may also be receiving additional pensions and other interest on which tax has been deducted. Again, many will be entitled to tax refunds (see Chapter 12 on page 110).

To claim a tax refund

Write to any tax office asking for leaflet IR110. This gives you some helpful information and, in particular, the leaflet contains a form for you to fill in and return to your tax office requesting a tax refund (see page 107 for further details).

Living abroad

If you retire abroad, you will still be liable to UK tax on any income you receive from the UK over and above your UK tax allowances; any income you receive abroad will be taxed according to that country's tax regulations. Some countries have a double taxation agreement with the UK, in which case you may get taxed under local tax regulations and not those of the UK. See page 57 as regards non-residency and period of visits to the UK.

You will also need to familiarise yourself with local legislation as regards inheritance tax and local forms of death duties.

As regards your social security, healthcare and pension rights, if you live in the European Community, contact the DSS overseas branch at Tyneview Park, Newcastle upon Tyne, NE98 1YX, who publish a free leaflet on these matters and can advise you on your personal situation.

CHAPTER 18

Money matters

As well as taking care of your family tax affairs, it is a good idea to know some of the best kinds of financial planning available, not only for the present but also for the future.

Refer to Chapter 17 on page 150 to ensure that you have allocated investments between partners to make the best use of the tax system.

Savings and investment opportunities

There are five important issues to consider when deciding where to invest your savings. Make sure that:

- You have some savings where you can get at your money quickly in an emergency.
- You are making full use of tax-free savings.
- You are not putting money into taxable investments where you are unable to reclaim, or offset, any tax deducted.
- You are not restricting social security benefits by getting income from investments.
- You are not taking unnecessary risks or, at least if you are, do ensure that you understand the full repercussions if things go wrong.

Various savings opportunities and their tax implications are now considered below.

Building society deposit or share accounts

These combine safety with easy access and a flexible rate of interest. They are particularly useful if you are saving for eventual house purchase as building societies tend to give preference to existing investors.

Interest is paid after having the tax deducted at the rate of 20 per cent. If your total income is unlikely to exceed your personal allowance you can fill in form R85, and once the building society receive this completed form they will pay interest gross (see page 116).

Note, however, that cash windfalls on a building society takeover/ conversion may be liable to capital gains tax and a cash windfall on a merger may be liable to income tax.

Bank deposit accounts
Banks are now more flexible in the variety of deposit accounts and interest you can have to suit your particular needs. The interest has tax deducted at the rate of 20 per cent, but non-taxpayers can receive payments gross by filling in the appropriate form (see building society accounts above).

Offshore accounts
Many people invest in offshore building society or bank accounts in order to benefit from receiving interest gross and paying tax later. Such cash flow advantage can be lost, however, if you have to make tax payments on account during the year under self assessment. Also, there could be repayment delays and local probate problems in the event of death.

You must tell your tax office if you open an offshore account, otherwise you could face penalties.

The interest must be declared on your tax return and, under the European Savings Directive which came into force on 1 July 2005, banks within the EU and certain other countries are required to report details of the income you receive from overseas accounts to the tax office.

You either have to agree to let the bank tell the tax authorities about the interest or suffer a 15 per cent withholding tax.

In addition, certain countries or territories which were reluctant to comply with the information-exchange requirements of the directive have opted instead to withold tax on interest payments; these countries include Jersey, Guernsey and the Isle of Man.

National Savings and Investments
There is a helpline on 0500 007 007 and a website **www.nsandi.com**. On that website there is a 'Help me to decide' section that takes you through the various options and can be very useful. Current interest rates are also updated regularly.

National Savings easy access savings account
Like a building society account, this is an easy method of saving and money is easily withdrawn. Interest is paid gross but is still taxable and should be shown in your tax return.

These accounts replaced the National Savings ordinary accounts, which are now closed for transactions. Savers with existing ordinary accounts should have received a letter from National Savings and Investments suggesting they transfer their account into this new type of account.

National Savings direct saver accounts
These accounts can only be managed online or by telephone. Interest is paid gross but is taxable and should be shown in your tax return.

National Savings investment account
These accounts offer a tiered interest rate depending on the amount in the account. Interest is paid gross but is still taxable and should be shown in your tax return.

National Savings certificates
There are two types of certificates: fixed interest and index linked. With both types interest is added to your capital and paid at the end of a five-year period. Interest is free of income tax and capital gains tax and you do not have to declare it in your tax return. If you do have to cash in a certificate before the expiry date then you will lose part of your interest but your capital will be secure.

National Savings income bonds
These are designed for savers who wish to receive regular monthly payments of interest whilst at the same time preserving the full cash value of their investments. The interest is paid monthly without tax being deducted. However, the interest is taxable and should be declared in your tax return.

National Savings guaranteed income, growth and equity bonds
No issue of these three types of bond is currently on sale. Interest earned on existing issues is liable to tax.

National Savings Children's bonus bonds
A high-interest savings scheme for children under the age of 16. Interest is added on each anniversary plus a bonus on the fifth anniversary. Both the interest and bonus is tax free and parents can fund these without affecting their own tax liability.

Premium bonds
No interest is paid but a draw is held monthly for varying cash prizes. All prizes are tax free and do not have to be shown in your tax return.

Individual savings accounts (ISAs)
All income and capital gains arising from these accounts is free of tax (except from dividends on share ISAs where the 10 per cent tax credit will have been deducted from the dividend before you receive it, and cannot be reclaimed). Interest received on a cash ISA does not have to be shown on your tax return. Note that you do not get any relief for any loss that you may make on an ISA investment.

The annual amount you can invest in an ISA for 2011–2012 is £10,680 – up to one half of which can be invested in a cash ISA (i.e. a savings account) and up to one half in a stocks and shares ISA. Always check with your ISA provider as to the rules and regulations as they can vary. There is an HMRC savings helpline on 0845 604 1701.

Friendly societies
The maximum you can invest in a savings plan for the interest to be tax exempt is £270 a year if paid in a lump sum or £300 if paid monthly.

Unit trusts
These are a way for the small investor to benefit from investing in a wide range of companies. Many trusts nowadays specialise in different areas of investment – some with emphasis on capital growth, or income, or overseas companies, or property (such as REITS and property AIFs). You can purchase units directly from the unit trust company, or through a bank or broker. You pay tax on the income and gains in the normal way.

Purchased life annuities
These are covered in the Pensioners chapter on page 117.

Endowment policies
Many people took out this form of insurance policy, often to cover a possible contingency like paying off a mortgage or celebrating early retirement, but often the policy was not cashed in but continues to exist after its original purpose has perhaps become obsolete.

There is a sound financial market now for selling on these policies and you should get quotations from a professional advisor – contact the Association of Policy Market Makers 0845 833 0086, **www.apmm. org**. Financially it is usually best to hold onto a policy until maturity, especially if you are getting tax relief, which is available only on pre14 March 1984 policies.

Finance houses
These are businesses which generally pay a higher rate of interest than the average market rate. It is important to consult an accountant or solicitor or financial adviser to obtain an opinion as to a particular finance house's financial stability.

Permanent interest-bearing shares (PIBs)
These are building society shares which are listed on the stock exchange and are traded on the stock market. There is a fixed rate of interest. They are not as secure as gilt-edged investments or building society accounts, and they are not as marketable when you wish to sell.

Bonds

The bond market has expanded rapidly over the last few years with many variations such as investment bonds, guaranteed income bonds, fixed-rate bonds, etc. They are methods of investing lump sums. Watch carefully for hidden charges that could eat into your capital and bear in mind that you could lose if interest rates rise and you are locked into a fixed rate over a number of years. Tax is deducted from the interest when it is paid and cannot be reclaimed by non-taxpayers.

Government stocks

These stocks, known as gilt-edged securities, are quoted on the stock exchange. They can be purchased through a bank or broker or direct from the Gifts Register (**www-uk.computershare.com** or telephone 0870 703 0143).

Interest is paid gross but if you do want to have tax deducted from your interest you can elect to do so when you buy the shares. Profits on sale are free from capital gains tax.

Ordinary shares in quoted companies

Buying shares quoted on the stock exchange is a gamble, for the share price of even the most well-known names can fluctuate considerably over a short period. You should obtain professional advice before investing.

Dividends are paid after allowing for a tax credit.

If you are a non-taxpayer, this tax credit cannot be reclaimed and it may be more beneficial to put savings into investments that pay gross interest without any tax deductions.

The amount of dividend received, plus the tax credit, has to be added to your total income in working out your overall tax liability and if this takes you into the higher rate band, then more tax will be payable. If you are a basic rate taxpayer, there is no further liability.

Enterprise investment scheme (EIS)

Under these schemes, an individual can gain tax relief on investments in unquoted trading companies. The main provisions are as follows:

- Income tax relief is given at 30 per cent (20 per cent for 2010–2011) on qualifying investments up to £500,000 per year. This is to be increased to £1 million from April 2012.

- Gains on disposal are exempt from capital gains tax.

- There is income tax or capital gains tax relief for losses on disposal.

- Eligible shares must be held for at least three years, otherwise you will lose the tax relief.

The rules and regulations governing these schemes are very complex. Do seek professional advice before investing.

Venture capital trusts

These were introduced to encourage individuals to invest indirectly in unquoted trading companies.

The main provisions are:

1. Individuals are exempt from tax on dividends arising from shares acquired in these trusts, up to £200,000 a year.

2. Income tax relief of 30 per cent on up to £200,000 in any tax year for subscribing for new shares.

3. Gains arising on the disposal of shares are free of capital gains tax.

There is useful reference material available from the British Venture Capital Association on 020 7420 1800, **www.bvca.co.uk**.

Community investment relief

Investments made by individuals and companies in a community development finance institution qualify for tax relief of 5 per cent a year of the investment for a period of five years.

Investing in property

Investing in a second property may provide a safe investment over a *longer* period, even though any profit you might make on selling would be subject to capital gains tax. For tax relief on interest on borrowing for such a purpose, see page 89 and for the tax treatment of property income see page 86.

Selling your house

Any profit you make on selling the property you own and live in is free from capital gains tax. See page 140 for the capital gains tax position where there is an overlap between buying and selling, and the situation regarding letting; also using your home for business.

Charitable giving

There are many ways of giving to charity tax efficiently and these are all covered in Chapter 8 on page 91.

Pension schemes

In general, contributing to a pension scheme is a good idea because:

1. You currently get tax relief at your top income tax rate on the contributions.

2. The pension scheme will provide you with additional income to supplement your State pension when you retire.

3. A tax-free capital sum can be taken on retirement, and sometimes before retirement depending on the rules of your pension scheme.

4. Employer's contributions to your scheme are not treated as a taxable benefit.

However do bear in mind that there is no guarantee that pension funds will increase in value in the short term – they are essentially long-term investments. Unregistered pension schemes to not qualify for tax relief status.

How do you get tax relief on pension contributions?

1. If you are in an occupational pension scheme, your employer will deduct your contribution from your salary before PAYE tax is calculated – that way you will get tax relief at your highest tax rate.

2. If you are a member of a personal pension scheme or a stakeholder scheme (these have a cap on management charges), basic rate tax is deducted when you pay the net premium; if you are a higher or additional rate taxpayer you can claim the difference between that rate and the basic rate in your tax return.

3. For most retirement annuity contracts you will pay the premium gross and you can claim tax relief in your tax return – although sometimes your PAYE tax code will have been adjusted to take the relief into account.

There is no limit as to the amount you can pay into a pension plan, unless you have zero earnings in which case the maximum for tax relief is £2,880 a year (HMRC will add another £720 as tax relief to make it up to £3,600 a year). There is no limit to the number of plans you can have but there are restrictions on the amount of tax relief you can claim.

Limits for tax relief

There are two main restrictions that limit tax relief – an Annual Allowance limit and a Lifetime Allowance limit (see table below):

Pension allowances		
Tax year	Annual allowance £	Lifetime allowance £
2006–2007	215,000	1,500,000
2007–2008	225,000	1,600,000
2008–2009	235,000	1,650,000
2009–2010	245,000	1,750,000
2010–2011	255,000	1,800,000
2011–2012	50,000	1,800,000

Annual allowance

These figures include your contributions and your employer's contributions and, in the case of salary-related schemes any increase in your pension multiplied by 16 (prior to 6 April 2011 the figure was 10) plus any increase in your right to a lump sum. Any excess over the maximum amounts shown in the table will be taxed at your top rate of tax but if you have not used your full allowance in the previous three years then you can claim any unused allowance in the current year.

Lifetime allowance

How do you calculate the value of your lifetime allowance? You add together the value of any money purchase schemes, plus the annual pension of any final salary scheme multiplied by 20 plus any benefits already drawn.

You can protect your lifetime allowance at £1.8 million (the maximum reduces to £1.5m for 2012) if you apply to your tax office by 5 April 2012, provided you make no further contributions.

If you exceed the lifetime allowance limits, then when you take benefits you will have to pay tax on the excess at the rate of 55 per cent on any lump sum withdrawals and 25 per cent if you draw an income (additionally the income will be taxed when you receive it)

Pension schemes – general considerations

When you are considering your pension rights both as regards tax-free lump sum payments and annuity or drawdown options do ensure that you get detailed quotes, not only from your current pension scheme provider but also from other companies for they do vary considerably from company to company. This is known as your open-market option – you do not have to stay with your existing provider.

From a tax point of view, remember that any pension income has to be added to your State pension and all your other income, to arrive at your total income for tax purposes, and this figure will determine what PAYE tax code will be applied to your private pension income because the provider of that pension will deduct tax before paying your pension.

If you are a member of your employer's salary-related occupational pension scheme your scheme's administrator will give you information on any tax-free lump sum available and the pension amount you will receive. For money purchase schemes you will have to get quotations as mentioned above.

Your pension scheme will define the earliest age at which you can retire but since 6 April 2010 every pension scheme cannot have a minimum retirement age earlier than 55 in order to draw tax advantaged benefits. There may be exceptions if you are in bad health. You don't have to stop work to draw pension benefits from a personal pension scheme.

Tax-free lump sums
You can take a tax-free cash lump sum from a pension scheme of up to 25 per cent, subject to the rules of your scheme, even if you carry on working but there is a maximum limit of £450,000 for 2011–2012 and £375,000 for 2012–2013.

Triviality payments
If your pension scheme is valued at less that £18,000 (in 2011–2012), you are over 60 and under 75 years of age, then you can take the whole sum in cash; 25 per cent will be tax free and the balance will be taxed as income.

Your pension scheme retirement options
Only a general overview is given here so it is important to consult a professional advisor.

In the case of money purchase schemes there are basically two options.

Option one
Use your pension fund, less any cash lump sum taken, to buy a lifetime annuity. There are various types of annuities. For example you can build in an inflation factor, or have a guaranteed minimum period whereby the annuity continues for a period after your death, or you can have a joint annuity whereby your partner continues to receive

an income after your death. Do ensure you get several quotes from insurance companies and explore all the various options particularly if you suffer from any health problems.

Option two

Leave your pension fund intact and draw an income as you need it – called 'income drawdown'. Prior to 6 April 2011 you had to take an annuity once you were over 75 years of age but this regulation was removed in the budget.

The amount of income drawdown you can take is limited to the open market value of an annuity so it will depend on your age and market conditions – your pension advisor will give you the figures. If you have at least £20,000 of income per year from other pension schemes, including the State pension, then this restriction is waived.

What happens to pension schemes and annuities on death

If you die when you are still in service then it will depend on the terms of the pension scheme as to the death benefits that will pass to your estate.

If you were in receipt of an annuity then there will be no capital sum to pass on to your family when you die. Obviously the annuity payment may continue for the benefit of your partner if it was in joint names or was for a guaranteed period.

If you had been taking income drawdown so that there remains a capital sum in the pension fund then this capital sum can pass to your estate but will suffer a tax charge of 55 per cent but with inheritance tax exemption on the pension monies paid out. (The figures prior to 6 April 2011 were 35 per cent up to age 75 and 82 per cent above that age.) You can avoid this tax charge if you leave the sum to charity, or if it is used to provide a drawdown pension for a dependant, or if you die before aged 75 before drawing any benefits.

Useful contact numbers

Two useful reference sources are the Office of the Pension Advisory Service (OPAS) – their website is **www.opas.org.uk** and there is a helpline specifically for women on 0845 600 0806. Additionally refer to **www.hmrc.gov.uk/pensionschemes**.

Other pension schemes

A self-invested personal pension (known as SIPPs) and small self-administered schemes (known as SSASs) are governed by the same pension rules detailed above, the main difference is that you have a wider range of investments to choose from rather than being restricted to those of an insurance company.

Other pension issues

Insolvency and pensions
Anyone filing for bankruptcy does not have to include any personal pension fund in their statement of assets, except where fraud could be established. Legislation already exists to protect money saved in occupational pension schemes from creditors and new legislation is currently being enacted which will give some protection to pension rights if an employer becomes insolvent.

Part-timers and pension rights
Following recent legislation, anyone who has been prevented from joining an occupational pension scheme because of their part-time status can have pension rights backdated to 1976. Such employees must, however, still be working for the relevant company or lodge a claim within six months of leaving.

Divorce and pension rights
The law allows for the allocation of pension funds and rights at the divorce date between husband and wife. However, this does not happen automatically and it needs to be discussed with your solicitor as part of the divorce settlement negotiations.

If your pension provider goes out of business
The Pension Protection Fund and the Financial Assistance Scheme both exist to grant compensation to members of pension schemes that go out of business, or whose members have lost out due to their scheme being underfunded and the employer becoming insolvent, or where they no longer exist. Go to the following sites for information: **www.dwp.gov.uk** or **www.pensionprotectionfund.org.uk**.

How to trace old pension schemes
Either contact your former employer or, failing that, contact the Pension Schemes Registry on 0870 606 3636. They also have a website at **www.thepensionsregulator.gov.uk**.

State pension forecast
You can write to the Pension Service Retirement Pension Forecast Unit at Tyneview Park, Newcastle upon Tyne NE98 1BA to get a forecast of your likely State pension and SERPS entitlements.

There is also a telephone number 0845 300 0168 and a website at **www.thepensionservice.gov.uk**.

CHAPTER 19

Calculating your own tax and the *Check Your Tax* calculator

If you want to calculate your tax when you send in your tax return, you need to ask for the tax calculation summary pages – telephone 0845 9000 404.

All the boxes are numbered according to the boxes in the main tax return and any supplementary pages that you need to complete, and although these forms look very complicated it is really a question of transferring all the figures into the correct summary boxes and following the instructions to ensure that you do the additions and subtractions according to the sequence. Because the tax office have to cover all possible tax situations, their working sheets are very comprehensive and lengthy.

You may find it more convenient to use the *Check Your Tax* calculator on the following pages; even if you don't want to do your own tax you may find the calculator useful to check the statements you get from the tax office.

Use the tax return working notes on pages 173–180 to jot down individual figures or use for calculations.

Check Your Tax calculator

This layout is designed for the year ended 5 April 2011 but you could use it for earlier years provided you alter the tax rates and include the correct allowances (see page 186).

   Do not include any income that is tax free (for example, ISAs or National Savings certificate interest) – see pages 13–15.

Check Your Tax calculator	Tax deducted	Gross amount
Your non-savings income		
Salary or wages after deducting any pension scheme contribution or payroll giving	....	....
State pension		....
Other pensions	....	....
Benefits from employer (see form P11D)	....	....
Profits from self-employment (usually the accounts period ending in the 2010–2011 tax year) or freelance earnings, after capital allowances and loss relief		....
Casual earnings, after expenses	....	....
Social security benefits that are taxable		....
Income from land and property, after expenses (exclude tax-free rental under rent-a-room scheme)	....	....
Total non-savings income	(a) £	(A) £ ....
Less: Allowable expenses		
Personal pension contributions, including retirement annuity contribution for this year (exclude any contributions deducted from salary under PAYE above)	....	....
Market value of shares etc. and land and buildings gifted to charities		....
Interest paid on qualifying loans	....	....
Other expenses allowed for tax	....	....
Total allowable expenses	(b) £	(B) £ ....
Savings income (excluding dividends)		
Interest received	....	....

	Tax deducted	*Gross amount*
Dividend income		
Dividends received (you should add the tax credit to this and then show it separately in the tax-deducted column)	....	....
<u>Total savings and dividend income</u>	(c) £	(C) £ ....
<u>Total income and tax deducted</u> a–b+c=(d) £		(D) £ ....
		A-B+C=D

Less: Allowances claim

Personal allowance/age allowance
(but deduct any income limit
reduction if over 65
– see table on page 186) ....

Blind person's allowance ....

<u>Income on which tax is payable</u>

   (D minus total allowances)   (E) £ ....

Tax payable

  (see band limits on page 186 and notes below)

Non-savings income (see note 4)

£	at 10 per cent (see note)	....
£	at 20 per cent	....
£	at 40 per cent	....
£	at 50 per cent	....

Savings income

£	at 20 per cent	....
£	at 40 per cent	....
£	at 50 per cent	....

Dividend income

£	at 10 per cent	....
£	at 32.5 per cent	....
£	at 42.5per cent	....

(E) £................   Total (F) ....

Less: Your claim for personal allowances
that are available at only 10 per cent

Married couple's allowance ....
(but note any restriction
– see page 95)

Maintenance or alimony
(max £2,670) ....

(G) £ ....@ 10 per cent =   (H) £ ....

(F–H=I) £ ....

Less: Relief at the appropriate percentage for:

Enterprise investment scheme ....

Venture capital trust ....

Community investment ....

£ ....   = (J) £ ....

Less: Tax already deducted   (d) £ ....

Tax due (or refundable if this is a minus figure) I – J – d = K   (K) £ ....

Notes:
1. You cannot reclaim the 10 per cent tax credit on dividends.
2. You will need to add to the tax due, any Class 4 national insurance liability, any capital gains tax liability and any underpayment from a previous year. (Deduct any tax repayment already received or any potential underpayment already in your tax code for a later year).
3. Your total tax liability will need to be adjusted for any carry back of gift aid.
4. The basic-rate band will be increased by the gross amount of any gift aid.

Allocation of tax rate bands
The sequence in which you calculate your tax rates is critical to the way the tax system works – refer to the sequence list on page 105.
You are taxed at 20 per cent on the first £37,400 of earned or pension income, or 20 per cent of savings income, and 10 per cent on dividend income. Note, however, that you may be eligible for the starting savings rate of 10 per cent on all or some of your non-dividend savings income (see page 104).
After that, you pay 40 per cent on net income up to £150,000 and 50 per cent above that figure except dividend income, which is charged at 32.5 per cent or 42.5 per cent (see page 186).

CHAPTER 20

Tax return working notes

U se these boxes to make a note of how you compiled the figures that you put in your tax return or as a memory jogger.

Interest and dividends received

Property income and expenses

Other income

Earnings and benefits

Expenses claimed

Car details and car mileage notes

Pension income and pension scheme notes

Gift aid donations

Capital gains notes

Inheritance tax notes

Useful reference numbers

Taxation, tax credits and national insurance

Child tax credit claim line and helpline: 0845 300 3900

Construction industry helpline: 0845 366 7899

Construction industry order line: 0845 366 7899

HM Revenue and Customs main website: **www.hmrc.gov.uk**

HM Revenue and Customs pension scheme helpline: 0115 974 1600

HM Revenue and Customs pension scheme website:
   www.hmrc.gov.uk/pensionschemes

National insurance helpline for employees: 0191 225 3002

National insurance helpline for employers: 0845 714 3143

National insurance helpline for the self-employed: 0845 915 4655

Pension credit helpline: 0800 99 1234

Requests for tax forms and help sheets: 0845 9000 404

Tax and the self-employed helpline 0845 915 4515

Tax office helpline: 0845 9000 444 Taxback helpline: 0845 077 6543

Savings and pensions, etc.

Association of policy market makers (endowment policies)
   0845 833 0086

British Venture Capital Association: 020 7420 1800, **www.bvca.co.uk**

Child trust fund help: 0845 302 1470, **www.childtrustfund.gov.uk**

Law societies for England and Wales: 020 7242 1222

Law societies for Northern Ireland: 0289 023 1614

Law societies for Scotland: 0131 226 7411

National Savings and Investments: 0500 007 007, **www.nsandi.com**

Office of the pension advisory service: 0845 600 0806,
   www.opas.org.uk

Pension schemes registry: 0870 606 3636

Pension service: 0800 99 1234, **www.thepensionservice.gov.uk**

Society of trust and estate practitioners: 020 7340 0500

Your Pension Choice booklet: 0845 731 3233

Personal tax data record

National insurance number ....

State pension number ....

Tax reference number..

Tax office address ....

Tax office telephone number ....

2009 tax return sent ....

2009 tax return assessment agreed ....

2010 tax return sent ....

2010 tax return assessment agreed ....

2011 tax return sent...

2011 tax return assessment agreed ....

Notes on correspondence ....

....

....

....

....

....

....

....

....

....

....

....

....

....

....

....

....

Contacts and location of documents checklist

Accountant's name and address ....

....

Bank name and address ....

....

Solicitor's name and address..

....

Birth, marriage and divorce certificate location ....

....

Car documents, data, contacts and location ....

....

Insurance policy data, contacts and location ....

....

Pension scheme data, contacts and location ....

....

Property/mortgage deeds data, contacts and location ....

....

Share and investment certificates location ....

....

Trust deeds location ....

....

Wills held by ....

....

Working tax credit, child tax credit and child benefit

There are numerous elements making up these tax credits as indicated in Chapter 9.

Note that you will receive a higher rate of working tax credit if you are aged 50 or more and have just returned to work after qualifying for out-of-work benefits; or you are a working person disadvantaged from getting a job because of a disability; or you have a severe disability.

If you are eligible for the working tax credit and you pay a registered or approved child minder to look after your child and you work at least 16 hours a week, you may be able to get a contribution of up to 70 per cent of your costs paid through the working tax credit scheme.

The figures below are per year unless stated otherwise.

Working tax credit	2010–2011 £	2011–2012 £
Basic element	1,920	1,920
Couple and lone parent element	1,890	1,950
30 hour element	790	790
Disabled worker element	2,570	2,650
Severe disability element	1,095	1,130
50+ Return to work payment (16–29 hours)	1,320	1,365
50+ Return to work payment (30+ hours)	1,965	2,030

Childcare element of the working tax credit		
Maximum eligible cost for one child	£175 per week	£175 per week
Maximum eligible cost for two or more children	£300 per week	£300 per week
Percentage of eligible costs covered	80 per cent	70 per cent

Child tax credit		
Family element	545	545
Family element, baby addition	545	0
Child element	2,300	2,555
Disabled child element	2,715	2,800
Severely disabled child element	1,095	1,130

Income thresholds and withdrawal rates

	2010–2011	2011–2012
	£	£
First income threshold	6,420	6,420
First withdrawal rate (per cent)	39%	41%
Second income threshold	50,000	40,000
Second withdrawal rate (per cent)	6.67%	41%
First threshold for those entitled to child tax credit only	16,190	15,860
Income disregard	25,000	10,000

Child benefit and guardian's allowance rates

	2010–2011	2011–2012
	£ per week	£ per week
Eldest/only child	20.30	20.30
Other children	13.40	13.40
Guardian's allowance	14.30	14.75

APPENDIX 5

Residential stamp duty

	Total value consideration	
Rate	2010–2011	2011–2012
0%	Up to £125,000	Up to £125,000
1%	£125,001–250,000*	£125,001–250,000*
3%	£250,001–500,000	£250,001–500,000
4%	over £500,000	£500,001–1,000,000
5%		over £1,000,000

*First-time buyers can claim a zero rate on up to £250,000 consideration for purchases between 25 March 2010 and 24 March 2012.

Refer to www.whatmortgage.co.uk where you can calculate how much stamp duty will be levied.

Rates of tax and allowances

	2011–2012	2010–2011	2009–2010
Income tax			
Savings starting rate at 10 per cent	£2,560	£2,440	£2,440
Basic rate at 20 per cent	£0–£35,000	£0–£37,400	£0–£37,400
Higher rate at 40 per cent	over £35,000	over £37,400	over £37,400
Additional rate at 50 per cent	over £150,000	over £150,000	–

The starting rate for savings income is not applicable if an individual's taxable non-savings income is above this limit.

Dividend income is taxed at 10 per cent for basic rate taxpayers, 32.5 per cent for higher-rate taxpayers and 42.5 per cent for additional-rate taxpayers.

Capital gains tax			
Exemption limit – individuals	£10,600	£10,100	£10,100
Exemption limit – trustees	£5,300	£5,050	£5,050
Tax rate (basic rate)	18 per cent	18 per cent	18 per cent
Tax rate (higher rate)	28 per cent	18 per cent before 23-06-2010 28 per cent after 23-06-2010	18 per cent

Inheritance tax			
Exemption limit	£325,000	£325,000	£325,000
Tax rate	40 per cent	40 per cent	40 per cent
Personal allowance	**£7,475	**£6,475	£6,475
Age allowance			
Aged 65–74 personal	£9,940	**£9,490	£9,490
Aged 75+ personal	£10,090	**£9,640	£9,640
married couple's	£7,295	*†£6,965	*†£6,965
Minimum amount	£2,800	*£2,670	*£2,670
Income limit	£24,000	£22,900	£22,900

**From April 2010 the personal and age allowance will be gradually withdrawn for income over £100,000 per year at a rate of £1 of allowance lost for every £2 over £100,000, until it is completely removed.

Blind person's allowance	£1,980	£1,890	£1,890
Corporation tax			
Full rate	26 per cent	28 per cent	28 per cent
Small companies rate	20 per cent	21 per cent	21 per cent

Notes: *Relief restricted to 10 per cent. †If born before 6 April 1935.

Index